Instructor's Manual for
A Practical Guide to Behavioral Research

Instructor's Manual for

A Practical Guide
To Behavioral Research
Tools and Techniques

THIRD EDITION

Barbara Sommer
Robert Sommer

New York   Oxford
OXFORD UNIVERSITY PRESS
1991

Oxford University Press

Oxford   New York   Toronto
Delhi   Bombay   Calcutta   Madras   Karachi
Petaling Jaya   Singapore   Hong Kong   Tokyo
Nairobi   Dar es Salaam   Cape Town
Melbourne   Auckland

and associated companies in
Berlin   Ibadan

Published by Oxford University Press, Inc.,
200 Madison Avenue, New York, New York 10016

Oxford is a registered trademark of Oxford University Press

ISBN 0-19-507152-2

9 8 7 6 5 4 3 2 1

Printed in the United States of America
on acid-free paper

Table of Contents

Preface 2

Section 1 Practical exercises 3

Section 2 Test bank 21

Chapter 1 Multimethod approach 21

Chapter 2 Ethics in behavioral research. 25

Chapter 3 How to do a literature review. 27

Chapter 4 Observation. 30

Chapter 5 Behavioral mapping and trace measures. 34

Chapter 6 Experimentation. 38

Chapter 7 Simulation 48

Chapter 8 Interview. 50

Chapter 9 The questionnaire. 55

Chapter 10 Attitude and rating scales 61

Chapter 11 Content analysis 70

Chapter 12 Personal documents and archival measures . . . 73

Chapter 13 Case study 75

Chapter 14 Apparatus. 76

Chapter 15 Standardized tests and inventions. 77

Chapter 16 Sampling 82

Chapter 17 Descriptive statistics 87

Chapter 18 Inferential statistics 94

Chapter 19 Calculators and computers. 105

Chapter 20 Writing and reviewing a research report. 106

Chapter 21 After the report 109

Final Examination Questions 110

Preface

There are many ways to teach research methods depending upon class size, facilities, and student level. Our preference is for a class that is not too large (40 students or less, if possible), moveable chairs, and teaching in two-hour blocks. The small size allows personal supervision of projects, the portable chairs enable work groups to function, and two-hour blocks give time for planning modest projects, data collection, and analysis. Some projects involve groups while others are done individually. Ideally, there would be a library shelf available containing projects from previous classes. The original (paper) reports would be classified according to key words, method (observation, interview, experiment, etc.), and student name in a desktop computer directory. Students would be encouraged to check the previous reports before embarking on their own projects.

This instructor's manual is keyed to book chapters. The first section contains the practical exercises. Although each exercise is associated with a single chapter, it can also be used to demonstrate the value of a multi-method approach by conducting several projects using different methods in the same setting. As an example, there are numerous projects that can be done in a library in addition to reviewing earlier research on the topic. One can use a library for observational studies, by diagramming how people arrange themselves. One can also conduct interviews or questionnaire studies about the library. One might undertake experiments on library seating, for example, leaving various types of markers at empty seats, and seeing to what degree each marker reserves a space at times of peak library usage.

Following the practical exercises are multiple-choice and essay questions, also keyed to chapters, along with a concluding section containing a few comprehensive questions useful for testing general understanding and principles that cut across chapters. No attempt is made to provide an equal number of multiple-choice or essay questions for each chapter. Some chapters lend themselves more readily than others to essay questions, e.g., research ethics and library use. Chapters such as experimentation with a plethora of technical terms, are appropriate for multiple-choice questions, while the statistics chapters seem best suited for short answer questions.

We hope you find this manual useful. We would like to hear of your experiences teaching the methods class and/or using the Sommer and Sommer book. Feedback from students was important in writing the book, and feedback from instructors can make it better.

Our mail address is Department of Psychology, University of California, Davis, CA., 95616-8686.

Chapter 1. Multimethod Approach

1. Imagine that there is a school for the blind nearby and the pupils are willing to be participants in your research study. Think of the various research questions you might want to investigate. What combination of methods would best answer such questions?

2. Examine several recent issues of a behavioral research journal in your field of interest. Classify and tabulate the methods used in each of the studies.

3. The following two studies can be done either by interviewing social science faculty at a college or university or by consulting the articles written by these faculty.
   a. Based on your interviews or reading of articles, can you identify systematic differences between social science departments in the choice of research methods? If such differences exist, what might account for them?
   b. Based on your interviews or reading of articles, are there differences between the fields in the proportion of basic and applied research that is being done? If such differences exist, what might account for them?

Chapter 2. Ethics in Behavioral Research

As a member of the University Ethics Committee, the following proposals are submitted for your consideration. You can decide to accept each proposal as is, require modifications, or reject it.

1. A graduate student in experimental psychology is interested in the effects of anxiety on learning. He proposes to recruit volunteers from introductory psychology classes, who will receive small amounts of extra credit for their participation. Each person will be asked to learn several lists of words. During one set of trials, the person will receive small jolts of a harmless electric shock. To increase the subject's anxiety, the shock machine will be made to look more powerful than it is. A bright red sign will be painted on the side, reading "Danger: High Voltage." The researcher will wear rubber gloves and put vaseline on the subject's arm where the electrodes are to be attached. The shock machine has been tested and proven to be harmless.

Would you approve the study or ask for additional measures to minimize the risks or inconvenience to the subjects? What should the investigator tell the subjects about the experiment beforehand?

2. An anthropologist proposes to spend a year studying the drug subculture at the local high school. She has obtained the permission of the high school principal and the school board. She wants to talk with drug dealers and users and to observe the kinds of transactions that occur.

   What is your recommendation regarding this study? What safeguards should be used to protect the respondents and/or the investigator? Is the researcher obliged to inform police or school authorities regarding illegal activities?

3. Select the most recent issue of a major journal in your area of interest. Read the first five articles in this issue from the standpoint of research ethics. Were the ethical issues discussed specifically? Could the same information produced by the research have been obtained in some other way with less risk or inconvenience to the participants? Did the investigator employ fraud or deceit? If so, could the study have been done in some other way without deception?

4. Campus guidelines prohibit your committee from approving research on pregnant women unless there are very strict safeguards, including medical screening and a physician or nurse physically present during the testing. The psychology graduate student described in 1, who wants to study the effect of anxiety on learning, proposes to screen female volunteers by asking if they are pregnant. Several members of your research ethics committee object to this question as an invasion of privacy. What would be your recommendation on the matter?

Chapter 3. How To Do a Literature Review

1. Conduct a literature search on one of the following topics: (a) the effects of color on mood, (b) the relationship between income and mental illness, (c) the sexual behavior of rhesus monkeys, or (d) the effects of music on worker productivity.

2. Consult Psychological Abstracts and Sociological Abstracts in order to find articles published during the previous three years on one of the following topics: (a) the use of television as an instructional tool or (b) public attitudes toward aging and the elderly.

3. Compile a list of the names and addresses of five people to whom you might write for further information on one of the following topics: (a) the use of television as an instructional tool or (b) public attitudes toward aging and the elderly.

4

Chapter 4.   Observation

1. Test the Reasoner hypothesis. "A woman crosses her legs within 30 seconds of sitting down." See if this is the case. Need to consider sampling, gather control data on men, keeping track of clothing, i.e., skirt vs. slacks or shorts.

2. Types of cars in campus parking lots--e.g., makes, models, and years. May be able to compare faculty/staff parking areas with student areas. Tabulate bumper stickers or window decorations.

3. Student clothing--frequency of various forms of attire; jeans, casual slacks, shorts, skirts. etc.

4. Seating arrangements in the library as related to room density, lone individuals v. groups, gender, exam week, etc.

5. Class openers--behavior of faculty at beginning of class. How many offer a greeting versus immediate lecturing. Use variables of subject matter, sex, age, etc.

6. Behavior in laundromats--who separates light and dark clothes, by sex, age, location of laundromat, and any other variables of interest.

7. Pub behavior--for those of legal age. Group size, amount consumed, and time spent. Can also be done in coffee shops.

8. Can you identify a dominance order among a flock of chickens in a barnyard or pigeons in a city park? Does one bird typically intimidate others? What kind of display behavior or threats do you notice? Can you tell if these reflect the age or sex of the bird? How does your presence affect the behavior of the flock? Try to measure how close you can approach before the birds move away. Do they maintain a constant distance from people?

9. Choose an intersection that is frequently used by bicyclists, such as one near a school or park. For each cyclist, record age, sex, whether alone or in a group, the type of bicycle, and the use of hand signals. How often are left turns made from the curb lane and from the center lane? How do traffic conditions affect turning procedures? Note any danger spots or near-accidents.

10. Spend several hours observing a children's playground. Tabulate the amount of usage of each piece of equipment. Pay special attention to sex and age differences and to lone and group activities.

11. In the central business district of a major city, look at the mannikins in department stores. Test the hypothesis that male mannikins show more activity and dominance than female mannikins.

12. Record seating arrangements at a cafeteria during peak and non-peak hours. Examine the favored tables by different groups of people (wall v. non-wall, window locations, etc.), check to see the amount of mixing that occurs according to gender, ethnicity, age, etc.

13. Systematically tabulate seating patterns on public buses during non-rush hours. Determine the preference for seats in particular parts of the bus (front v. rear, or aisle v. window locations). As a bus begins to fill up, and people occupy seats next to others, determine if there are gender, age, and ethnicity effects.

14. People waiting in line tend to leave more space between themselves and someone wearing brightly-colored clothing, e.g., a bright red or yellow jacket. Students can photograph people waiting in line and estimate distances of people next-in-line to those wearing bright clothing and those wearing more subdued clothing. It can also be done as an experiment, with students taking a place in line according to an experimental plan wearing either bright or subdued clothing. Meaurements are made by another observer of the distance maintained by other people in line or photographs taken and analyzed later.

Chapter 5. Behavioral Mapping and Trace Measures

1. Sit at the rear during several classes in the same room or lecture hall. Diagram seating patterns and participation in the discussion. When you have collected records from several classes, look for regularities in seating and for areas of high and low participation.

2. Select an outdoor location frequently marked by graffiti. Classify the graffiti as to form and content. In regard to form, how much graffiti is written in cursive, how much is printed, how much is drawn? Is it in color or black and white, etc.? In regard to content, what are the themes? How many of the messages consist of people's names or initials, home towns or streets? Are the messages sexual or political?

3. Secure permission from someone to record his or her movements throughout an entire day. When you have done this, transfer your observational notes to an actual map.

4. Compare the graffiti in several different locations in the same building or complex. Is the type of graffiti similar in men's and women's restrooms in local restaurants? Compare graffiti in campus locations associated with different departments, such as Art, Engineering, Science, etc. Is graffiti associated with the Art Department more creative in terms of theme and use of drawings, as distinct from its content and style?

5. Follow shoppers as they proceed through a supermarket. Is there a standard route that people will take? Are there differences between those with shopping carts and hand baskets? Time how long people stay at a supermarket as related to age, gender, and group composition. Record form and content of interaction in the supermarket.

6. Map the behavioral ecology of a shopping mall. Using time sampling procedures, map those locations where different groups of people are found. Are there locations where teenagers hang out? If time is available for person-centered maps, record how long people stay in the shopping mall and what they do there.

7. Tabulate the amount of personalization on or next to faculty offices. How many faculty members display cartoons, decorations, or other items of personal expression? Are differences among faculty related to department, gender, and academic rank? Compare the offices of faculty members and administrators in terms of personalization of external walls.

8. Tabulate the amount of personalization of rooms in student residence halls. Compare the amount of external decoration (on the outside of the door) with the amount of internal personalization. Are design and art students more likely than students in other majors to personalize their rooms? Examine gender differences in both amount and type of wall decorations.

9. During an election period, tabulate the number and content of front yard signs, election posters, political bumper stickers, or other materials. Examine differences by neighborhood with reference to previous election results. Compare the number of lawn signs in election districts with the subsequent election results. Is the number of signs, posters, or bumper stickers in a neighborhood predictive of the election outcome for the district?

10. Using a time sampling procedure, record the clientele at video game arcades. Record the age, gender, group size, and ethnicity of the participants. Are there group preferences for particular video games?

Chapter 6. Experimentation

1. Two heads are better than one: Anagram problem-solving task, independent variable is group: one person vs. couples. Second independent variable is list type. Dependent variable=number of solutions within specified time period.

Names of flowers		Names of animals	
Stimulus	Solution	Stimulus	Solution
Fiodafld	Daffodil	Peltoane	Antelope
Laezaa	Azalea	Koemyn	Monkey
Yidas	Daisy	Swarul	Walrus
Atroicnan	Carnation	Aguraj	Jaguar
Crodhi	Orchid	Strumak	Muskrat
Almelica	Camellia	Fluboaf	Buffalo
Srate	Aster	Blaylaw	Wallaby
Pynas	Pansy	Leazleg	Gazelle
Smylsua	Alyssum	Phondil	Dolphin
Clail	Lilac	Uboicra	Caribou
Tainupe	Petunia	Ethecah	Cheetah
Wousfreln	Sunflower	Chrisot	Ostrich
Agidaren	Gardenia	Tereg	Egret
Steamicl	Clematis	Clame	Camel
Mijsane	Jasmine	Brinkcomdig	Mockingbird
Cusroc	Crocus	Henckic	Chicken
Pypop	Poppy	Choornisetr	Rhinoceros
Schukeloeny	Honeysuckle	Gruntaona	Orangutan

Names of Flowers		Names of Animals	
Stimulus	Solution	Stimulus	Solution
Nayhitch	Hyacinth	Evareb	Beaver
Aidalh	Dahlia	Ekretsantal	Rattlesnake
Ilagamno	Magnolia	Thleepan	Elephant
Chufais	Fuchsia	Crodon	Condor
Groimlad	Marigold	Ebenhoye	Honeybee
Ipult	Tulip	Inckumph	Chipmunk
Lotiev	Violet	Ogroanka	Kangaroo
Benearv	Verbena	Pigema	Magpie
Sluto	Lotus	Rirulesq	Squirrel

8

----

2. STROOP Color-Word effect: Present color names in ink of a different color. For example,

Word	Ink color
BLUE	green
BLACK	blue
RED	yellow

    Task: to name the ink color of the stimulus. Dependent variables: time to completion, number of errors (usually interference of the word). As a control condition, can perform task with word upside down, eliminating interference. Can run these as 2 conditions and counterbalance order of presentation.

    Alternative design: Demonstrate effects of practice on performance by going through different sets or different order of the same set (without using the upside-down condition).

3. Abstract and concrete words: Hypothesis - sensory words are learned more easily than abstract words.

    Instructions:
    a. 3 minutes to learn as many words as possible on the 1st list.
    b. Turn the page over.
    c. Wait 30 seconds
    d. Write down recalled words.
    e. Repeat the procedure with the other 3 lists.

Abstract	Concrete (visual)	Abstract	Concrete (auditory)
height	sunset	phrase	dog
fill	red	formula	car
send	tiger	deficit	hammer
theory	window	idea	bell
loss	glow	same	waterfall
ask	diamond	code	piano
certain	daisy	quantity	horn
said	chair	instant	motor
element	moon	sort	crow

    Alternative design: Present in mixed lists (i.e., combining abstract and sensory terms in same lists).

4. Taste testing: Arrange blind tastings.
    a. Preference comparisons among colas, sodas, mineral water.
    b. Other food products, e.g., organic vs. standard; different brands of canned goods, microwave popcorn brands, etc.
    c. Product identification, e.g., Coke vs. Pepsi, classic vs. new coke.

5. Design an experiment to test the hypothesis that presence of litter attracts more litter.

6. Other pastures seem greener. Is there any perceptual basis to homeowners' complaints that the neighbor's yard always looks better than theirs? Conduct a pilot study to determine whether the neighbor's yard does look better and, if so, attempt to explain the reasons.

7. Can cockroaches or beetles be conditioned? Construct a small T-shaped maze out of cardboard or wood. Gently capture several insects and mark them, using washable paint. Place them one at a time at the long end of the maze. At one of the arms, place a morsel of food. See if you can train some of the insects to turn right and others to turn left.

8. Throw darts with the preferred and non-preferred hand and compare the scores.

9. Assemble a list of pro and con statements about some social issue. If desired, the scale of attitude toward marijuana (Table 10-1) can be used, with Statement 5 (neutral) removed. Each student in the class administers the scale to several respondents who answer "agree" or "disagree" to each statement. For half the respondents, the student says "good" when a pro-marijuana answer is given. For the remaining respondents, the student says "good" when an anti-marijuana answer is given. The hypothesis can be tested whether the reinforcement (student saying "good") increases the amount of agreement with statements taking the same position.

10. This experiment involves two researchers, one of whom collects signatures or names on a petition. The second person is a confederate of the researcher who acts like a naive subject. In a public location where other people are present, the experimenter first approaches the confederate to request a signature. Half the time the confederate enthusiastically signs and the other half vociferously rejects the petition. The effect of the earlier endorsement or rejection on the next (true) subject is observed.

Chapter 7.   Simulation

1. In the company of a friend, walk through a building blindfolded. Write down your experience afterward. Try the same procedure again, both blindfolded and with earplugs. As information from one sense is reduced, notice what happens to the information from other senses.

2. Design a board game based on cooperation rather than competition. Try to make it both interesting and playable.

3. This exercise involves a number of people, each of whom plays a different role in a discussion of the pros and cons of filling a nearby marsh to create a large industrial park. Select people to fill each of the following roles: real estate agent, chamber of commerce official, union representative, city planning department head, resident of a small community living near the marsh, environmentalist, duck-hunting club official, and resident of a nearby community who wants the town kept small.

Chapter 8.   Interview

1. On campus, conduct a survey using unstructured interviews on satisfaction of various programs and services such as food service, intramural sports, library facilities, parking, academic advising, etc.

2. On campus, undertake structured interviews on satisfaction with the programs and services described in the above question.

3. Divide the class into two groups, one of them conducting open-ended interviews on a topic, such as satisfaction with campus facilities and programs, and the other group conducting structured interviews. Compare the types of answers found in the two types of interviews.

4. Conduct a depth interview on student definitions of personal success or choosing to be or not to be a parent.

5. Prepare an interview form for children on a current social issue. Pretest it on six children.

6. Find a group of people who are sharply divided on some controversial issue. Separate them into two subgroups, one that is strongly in favor and the other opposed to the issue. Ask each subgroup to independently construct an eight-item interview form (exclusive of items of background information) on the topic. Compare the types of questions people in each group feel are important.

7. Draw up an open-ended and a closed interview form on the same topic. Interview six people using each form. Compare the time taken to administer and tabulate the replies. Also compare the usefulness of the information derived from each type of interview.

8. Select a topic that is more familiar to your respondents than to you. This might be a sport or game you have never played, a sickness or disability you have never experienced, a job that is unfamiliar to you, a religion you know little about, and so on. With the help of people more knowledgeable than you on the topic, construct an interview form and pretest it with several respondents. How easy is it to construct an interview form on a topic you know little about?

9. Building custodians are often not seen during the day and have little interaction with daytime employees. However, they have specific ideas about other employees based on what they encounter as they clean the building. Interview the custodians in your building. What do they feel about employees in different parts of the building, which areas are the easiest and most difficult to clean, what do custodians think of their work, and what could other employees do to make the custodians' lot easier?

Chapter 9. Questionnaire

1. Design two forms of a questionnaire on a topic. Make one form open-ended and the other form closed. Administer each form to fifteen to twenty people. Tabulate and compare the replies on the two forms.

2. Construct a questionnaire on exam anxiety. Include questions about physical symptoms as well as interpersonal relations. Pretest your questionnaire on a group of students to eliminate unclear or ambiguous items. Which issues or topics work best with closed questions and which require open-ended questions?

3. Construct a questionnaire dealing with preferences in music or art.

4. Construct a questionnaire for college students on satisfaction with various programs and services, such as food service, recreation programs, intramural programs, library facilities, parking, etc.

5. Construct a questionnaire on computer dating.

Chapter 10.   Attitudes and Rating Scales

1. Scaling:

    a. Develop a Thurstone-type scale for measuring attitudes on a controversial issue.

    b. Convert the Thurstone-type scale into a Likert-type scale.

    c. Ask a group of people to complete both the Thurstone and the Likert-type scales. Compare the scores on the two scales. Do people with the highest scores on the Thurstone-type scale also have the highest scores on the Likert-type scale?

2. Develop and pretest a scale for measuring the quality of lighting in a building.

3. Is it true that a blindfolded person cannot identify the individual ingredients in a can of mixed fruit or mixed vegetables? Design a rating scale and experiment to test this.

4. Obtain semantic differential ratings from both men and women for several emotions, including love, jealousy, and fear. Tabulate the responses of men and women separately. Compute the averages for each scale.

5. Measure people's attitudes before and after seeing a film that takes a strong position on a controversial issue.

6. Request students to rate prominent politicians on semantic differential scales. Are there consistent differences between the political parties in ratings on the dimensions of value, activity, and strength? To what degree are the ratings of politicians on value dimensions related to the respondent's own political views?

7. Conduct a taste test comparing fresh and dried pasta, or between different types of beverages, e.g., different soft drinks or juices.

8. Develop a rating scale for use with perfumes. Try it out on several different perfumes and check the reliability of the ratings.

9. Develop a Likert scale on attitude toward seatbelt usage. Compare the results with students' self-reports of seatbelt use.

10. Develop a Likert-type attitude scale on computer dating.

Chapter 11.   Content Analysis

1. Prepare a classification scheme for the analysis of network television during the evening hours.

2. Compare the advertising in a newspaper or magazine that caters to a specific ethnic group with the advertising in a comparable publication for the majority audience. Look at the types of products and services offered, whether the advertisements are in English or another language, the identity of the models shown in the advertisements, and so on.

3. Compare the help wanted ads in a newspaper for the same day in 1950, 1970, and 1990. Look at the types of jobs offered, whether they specify men or women, educational requirements, salaries and fringe benefits, mentions of job security, and other factors.

4. Develop a classification scheme and compare cartoon humor in several magazines.

5. Select several popular magazines and classify the models used in cigarette or liquor ads. Check the reliability of each category in the classification system. Analyze model age, gender, social class, ethnicity, etc.

6. In cigarette ads in popular magazines, tabulate the percentage of cigarettes that show smoke and those that do not.

7. Develop various hypotheses about gender or group stereotypes in specialized magazines. For example, look at gender roles in illustrations in publications aimed at different age groups, e.g., children's magazines, teenage magazines, adult magazines.

8. Compare advertisements in professional journals for nurses and those for physicians.

9. Analyze different newspapers for the amount of space devoted to local, state, national, and international news, news v. features (special columns), amount of space devoted to advertising, etc.

10. Compare the content of the comics pages in several different newspapers for drama v. humor, the age of the people depicted, etc.

11. Conduct a content analysis of newspaper editorials over several years to see if there is political bias.

12. Examine the content, number, and length of commercials across time of day on a radio or TV station.

13. Examine program content (e.g., comedy, drama, violence, etc.) varied across time of day.

Chapter 12.   Personal Documents and Archival Measures

1. Compile your own dictionary of jail and prison slang. Check the card catalog at your library to find the shelves containing books about prisons or jails. Select 3 or 4 autobiographies by former inmates. Skim each book and write down the slang expressions that are used. These expressions are called prison argot, the special language of the prison. Try to guess the meaning of the word or phrase by the way it is used in the book and write this down next to the word. Do the same for a second or third book until your list has reached 25 terms. Then check your interpretations in the Dictionary of American Slang or Dictionary of American Underworld Lingo.

2. Analyze an exchange of letters. At your library, you will probably find several volumes of correspondence between famous individuals. Select one such book and prepare a list of scoring categories that could be used to make a content analysis of the letters. You might want to tabulate how many times a certain topic is mentioned, or how often the personal pronoun "I" is used, the length of the letter, or the form of address. Using your categories, compare the first and the last letters in the book to see whether the correspondence has changed over time.

3. Obtain the records on mental hospital admissions for the past ten years. Are there seasonal trends in admissions, e.g., more people admitted in the winter when it is difficult to live on the streets than at other times of the year?

4. Photograph albums provide many glimpses into the memorable moments of people's lives. See if you can obtain access to a personal photograph album that covers a period of at least ten years. Make a tabulation of the occasions on which the pictures were taken. How many were done on vacations? How many involve birthdays, anniversaries, marriages, or other personal celebrations? How many were taken indoors and how many outdoors? Tabulate the number of times people are shown with others and alone.

5. Ask several friends to keep records of the time they spend on the telephone over a full week. Each call should be recorded separately in terms of its length and whether it was incoming or outgoing. Compare your friends in terms of (1) the number of calls, (2) the average duration of each call, and (3) whether there is a difference between incoming and outgoing calls.

6. If they are available, examine the records of a university health service and counseling service to see if students are more likely to seek assistance before and during examination periods than at other times of the year.

7. Analyze the pattern of floor wear in a major public building. Look for scuff marks, carpet wear, faded tiles, cigarette burns, and so on.

8. Are people who buy cheap brands more likely to litter than those who buy expensive brands? Tabulate the amount and kind of litter in a park or campground or along the side of the road. A comparison study, if you don't mind getting dirty, would consist of examining the contents of nearby trash cans. How do the items discarded as litter compare with those placed in trash cans?

9. During an election campaign, select several districts with different political orientations. Count the number of posters and bumper stickers supporting each candidate. Compare these figures with the actual voting patterns. To what extent can posters and bumper stickers be used as guides to how people in the district are likely to vote?

10. Is the death penalty a deterrent to murder? Compare the rates in states with or without the death penalty. If there has been a recent change in the law regarding the death penalty in a jurisdiction, compare crime rates before and after the change.

Chapter 13. Case Study

1.   Interview local residents regarding a natural hazard in the area,—e.g., a drought, fire, flood, or earthquake. Do they feel it likely that such an event will occur again? Have they made any preparations? Are natural hazards a significant factor in the decision to remain in the area?

2.   Select a person who is a friend of someone you know, but whom you do not know personally. Have your friend obtain the subject's permission to conduct a case study. It will be more interesting if you have never met the subject yourself. Interview people about the subject. Construct a picture of the subject's life from your interviews. If several students independently prepare case studies on this same person, the accounts can be compared. How do the personalities and interests of the people compiling a case study affect their accounts?

3.   Either based on newspaper accounts or your own knowledge of past events on campus, choose some incident that gained prominence, e.g., a residence hall fire, an altercation in a sports event, a rowdy party in which the police were called, etc. Interview the participants and compile a case study of the event. Remove any information from the report that might be used to identify individuals.

4.   Select a friend who agrees to be interviewed and explore in depth their attitudes, activities, and interests. Again with the person's permission, talk to their parents, siblings, and friends to gather additional information about these same items. Removing all information that might be used to identify the individual, write up a report integrating the various accounts of the person's life.

Chapter 14. Apparatus

This is an opportunity to introduce students to some of the apparatus available in the behavioral sciences. While this means a primary reliance on equipment that is available in a single department, there is also the possibility of borrowing equipment owned by another department or outside agency. The Student Health Service or a local optometrist may have color-blindness charts, the Physical Education Department various types of apparatus for testing reaction time, strength, endurance, etc. A communications or speech department may have equipment for measuring verbal interaction. A Human Development Department may have a fully equipped laboratory for observing and recording children's behavior. (continued)

Apparatus (cont.)

Some of these departments may be hospitable to an instructor's request for group usage of research equipment. Our Department of Food Science has been very receptive to requests for use of their sensory evaluation laboratory. One class used these facilities to compare tomatoes purchased at the farmers' market and supermarket. Another class compared classic with new Coke. Both these projects, incidentally, resulted in publications in the newsletter of a local food cooperative. The students were very pleased to see their work in print.

It is also possible to request the students to build or design simple items of behavioral equipment, as in Exercises 1 and 2 below.

1. A vertical line appears longer than a horizontal line of the same length. Construct an apparatus out of cardboard or paper to test this illusion. Measure the amount of distortion that occurs.

2. Design an apparatus that could be used to test whether cats are color-blind.

3. Using a camera with slide film, photograph a public area from a second or third story and analyze the distribution, density, and activity of people over time and according to weather conditions.

Chapter 15. Standardized Tests and Inventories

As with apparatus, the practical exercises will depend on the availability of tests for classroom use. Some tests will be easier than others to obtain. These will generally be tests that do not involve personal or sensitive information. Instructors may be able to order test kits and extra copies on their institutional letterhead or through the counseling center at a college or university. Many of these tests are suitable for classroom use, in that they are brief, do not elicit sensitive information, and have self-scoring keys. These tests can be demonstrated in class and then used by the students in a research study.

1. The Allport-Vernon-Lindzey study of values meets all of the above criteria, and is an interesting test for students to take. As a class research project, the responses of students majoring in different subjects (e.g., music, business, engineering, and chemistry) can be compared. On this and many other standardized tests, examine gender differences and differences between ethnic groups.

2. Administer a mood scale, such as the STAI (State-Trait-Anxiety Inventory) to students before and after an examination. Compare the scores of state anxiety and trait anxiety for the two time periods. See if there is any connection between changes that occur in the students' scores and their examination grades.

3. Obtain two forms of a test and administer it to the same group of students on different occasions. Correlate the scores to determine test reliability.

4. Administer a standardized test to a group of students. Randomly divide the test items in half and compute the split-half reliability coefficient for the two halves.

5. Administer two tests intended to measure similar constructs to a group of people, for example, two personality or interest tests. Correlate scores for similar scales on the two tests.

6. Using library sources such as the <u>Mental Measurement Yearbook</u>, assign teams of students the task of determining the reliability and validity of selected standardized tests. To what degree is validity and reliability information available and how useful does it appear to be?

7. Examine the published norms available for school achievement tests. To what degree do the samples reflect geographic and cultural diversity of the children who will be administered the test? Are the norms recent?

8. Request the students in the class to fill out a brief personality test measuring introversion and extroversion, such as the sub-scales of the Eysenck Personality Inventory or Myers-Briggs. Each student hands in the test with only a code number (no name) on it which is scored in class. Then the student approaches two friends or roommates and requests their ratings on his degree of introversion-extroversion along a seven-point scale. These are handed in to the instructor using the previous code number (no names). In class, compare the scores on the introversion-extroversion test with friends' ratings.

Chapter 16. Sampling

1. How would you select a sample of 100 children out of the 800 attending a junior high school in order to conduct a survey of political attitudes in this age group? Discuss some of the other methods that could be used for selecting children and why your method is preferable.

2. A department store has 200 employees, including 115 sales clerks, 60 stock clerks, delivery people, and maintenance employees, 20 supervisors, and 5 managers. For a study of employee morale, how would you choose (a) a random sample of 90 employees, (b) a stratified sample of 90 employees, and (c) a quota sample of 90 employees that will enable you to compare the morale at all levels in the organization?

3. To conduct a questionnaire survey of customer attitudes toward a restaurant chain, how would you select a sample of 300 customers? How would you go about finding a comparable sample of noncustomers to discover their attitudes toward the restaurant?

Chapter 17. Descriptive Statistics

Moore describes a brief and effective method for teaching students about measures of central tendency and reliability. Fifty straight, vertical lines, ranging from 21 to 99 mm were drawn parallel in random order on a 33 x 21 cm sheet. The fifty lines consisted of 25 different lengths; each length being represented by two lines. Lines of equal length were not adjacent. The lines were consecutively numbered from 1 to 50. In the right margin the numerals 1 through 50 appeared below one another, with enough space left to fill in measured length. Instructions at the top of the sheet asked the student to "Measure each line and record its length in the appropriate space on the right side of the page."

Copies of the sheet were given to students as a take-home assignment. They were told to measure each line and record its length on the sheet. The responses were tabulated and frequency distributions obtained for each line. The findings were then discussed in class.

For each line, the mean, mode, and median were compared to the line's true length. Reliability coefficients were computed in two ways. First, since each length appeared twice, parallel form reliability coefficients could be computed for each student. To obtain interjudge reliability coefficients, the responses of pairs of students for each line were correlated. Only 30 randomly selected pairs were used in these comparisons.

The instructor found the students intrigued by the task and surprised by the dispersion of obtained measurements.

End of Practical Exercises

Section 2: Test Bank

Chapter 1

Essay and Short Answers

Note: Numbers in parentheses refer to the page where the correct answer can be found.

A. Define the two different types of validity. (5-6)

B. Define the four types of research studies (basic, applied, instrumental, and action research) and the goals of the researcher in each case. (7)

C. List and briefly describe three (3) reasons for doing action research. (7)

D. What is meant by the method of <u>converging operations</u> and why is it important in research? (9)

E. Give an example of a cross-sectional and a longitudinal research study on the same topic. (14)

Multiple Choice

1.   The issue of whether the instruments or procedures measure what they are supposed to measure is called:
     a. evaluation research
     b. internal validity (5)
     c. reliability
     d. external validity
     e. program evaluation

2.   The generalizability of research findings is called:
     a. internal validity
     b. basic research
     c. reliability
     d. program evaluation
     e. external validity (5)

3.   External validity refers to whether the instruments measure:
     a. what they are supposed to measure
     b. whether the findings are repeatable
     c. whether a program is successful in solving real-world problems
     d. whether research findings are generalizable (5)
     e. whether the research is interdisciplinary

4. Internal validity refers to:
   a. the use of informants within a group converging operation
   b. whether the instruments or procedures measure what they are supposed to measure (5)
   c. repeatability of the findings
   d. the relevance of the findings to important theories of behavior

5. The repeatability of research findings is called:
   a. internal validity
   b. external validity
   c. internal operations
   d. external operations
   e. reliability (6)

6. Reliability refers to:
   a. the success of a program in meeting social needs
   b. the success of a program in answering long-range questions
   c. the repeatability of research findings (6)
   d. whether an instrument measures what it is supposed to measure
   e. the artificiality of experimental conditions

7. If research findings are reliable, they are:
   a. important
   b. useful
   c. valid
   d. invalid
   e. repeatable (6)

8. Providing answers to pressing questions is called:
   a. internal research
   b. instrumental research
   c. applied research (6)
   d. basic research
   e. behavioral research

9. Providing answers to long-range questions is called:
   a. action research
   b. evaluation research
   c. instrumental research
   d. basic research (6)
   e. behavioral research

10. Program evaluation is a type of
    a. applied research (6)
    b. instrumental research
    c. training exercise
    d. experimental research
    e. basic research

11. When a research study is done primarily to test a theory, it is probably:
    a. action research
    b. applied research
    c. basic research (6)
    d. instrumental research
    e. hypothetical research

12. Social psychologist Kurt Lewin developed a special type of research that combines the testing of theory with direct application. This is called:
    a. applied research
    b. experimental research
    c. action research (7)
    d. observational research
    e. contract research

13. Action research:
    a. seeks to evaluate existing programs
    b. mainly uses observational methods
    c. involves the potential users of the information in conducting the research (7)
    d. is primarily a training exercise
    e. is motivated primarily by the researcher's curiosity

14. For doing research on complex social problems, the textbook authors believe that behavioral research must use:
    a. program evaluation
    b. an interdisciplinary approach (8)
    c. natural observations
    d. field experimentation
    e. laboratory experimentation

15. When a number of different research techniques are used, each with somewhat different limitations and yielding somewhat different data, this is called the method of:
    a. synthetic research
    b. converging operations (9)
    c. experimental design
    d. practical experience
    e. action research

16. The best method for obtaining reliable information under controlled conditions is:
    a. personal interview
    b. laboratory experimentation (13)
    c. natural observation
    d. behavioral mapping
    e. psychological testing

17. The best method for finding out how people behave in public is:
    a. natural observation (13)
    b. personal documents
    c. interview
    d. questionnaire
    e. content analysis

18. The best method for finding out how people behave in private is:
    a. laboratory experimentation
    b. natural observation
    c. behavioral mapping
    d. psychological testing
    e. analysis of personal documents (13)

19. To learn what people think, the best method is:
    a. natural observation
    b. behavioral mapping
    c. laboratory experimentation
    d. interview (13)
    e. program evaluation

20. To identify personality traits or measure mental abilities, a researcher would probably use:
    a. psychological testing (13)
    b. laboratory experimentation
    c. field observation
    d. interview
    e. laboratory observation

21. A researcher studies the same group of high-achieving students over a 30-year period. This is called:
    a. behavioral mapping
    b. a person-centered map
    c. an experimental study
    d. an experiment-in-nature
    e. longitudinal research (14)

22. A researcher compares two groups of children on a test of hand coordination. This is a(n) _____ study.
    a. experimental
    b. observational
    c. basic research
    d. cross-sectional (14)
    e. applied research

Chapter 2
Essay and Short Answers

A. Discuss the reasons why universities and other organizations have developed procedures to protect human subjects in behavioral research studies. (16)

B. Describe some of the methods used by researchers to protect participants in behavioral studies. (20)

C. Two means of protecting respondents' privacy rights are <u>confidentiality</u> and <u>anonymity</u>. What is the difference between them? (20)

D. Discuss the pros and cons of using deception in behavioral research. (21)

E. Do you feel that the use of deception in behavioral research is ever justified? If so, discuss situations when you feel it is. If not, give your reasons why you feel it should not be used. (21)

Multiple Choice

1. Ethical guidelines are necessary in behavioral research:
   a. to ensure that the investigation used the correct procedures or instruments
   b. to provide feedback to the respondents
   c. to provide feedback to the researcher
   d. to protect the welfare of people serving as research subjects (16)
   e. to see that the research is both reliable and valid

2. The need for ethical review procedures in scientific research first came to public attention in:
   a. medical research (16)
   b. social psychological studies of obedience
   c. the Kinsey studies of sexual behavior
   d. studies of genetic engineering
   e. studies of crime and criminality

3. Two techniques used by researchers to protect participants in behavior research are:
   a. reliability and validity
   b. confidentiality and anonymity (20)
   c. reliability and converging operations
   d. personal documents and confidentiality
   e. all of the above

4. Under the principal of confidentiality:
   a. the respondent's identity is not known by the investigator
   b. the researcher provides information to government agencies without the public learning about it
   c. the researcher submits all relevant materials for review by a Human Subjects Committee
   d. the respondents' identity is known to the investigator but protected from public exposure (20)
   e. research grants are awarded without outside review

5. The best protection for people in an observational study is:
   a. confidentiality
   b. anonymity (20)
   c. reliability
   d. validity
   e. continuous evaluation

6. Behavioral researchers, like physicians, lawyers, and clergy, have a legal right to confidential communication. That is, their data are protected from legal scrutiny.
   a. true
   b. false (20)

7. The principle of anonymity means that:
   a. the researcher knows the identify of the participants but keeps this secret
   b. the researcher knows the identity of the participants and changes all names in the reports
   c. the researcher does not know the identity of the participants (20)
   d. the researcher keeps all sensitive information from reaching the public
   e. all of the above

8. Behavioral researchers _____ the special right to confidential communication acknowledged by the courts to physicians, lawyers, and the clergy.
   a. do have
   b. do not have (20)
   c. do not want

9. Most behavioral research involves _____ risk for human participants.
   a. little or no (21)
   b. some
   c. moderate
   d. considerable
   e. excessive

Chapter 3. How To Do a Literature Review

Essay and Short Answers

A. Describe the steps in a library search on a research topic (32).

B. You have looked up some references in the Psychological Abstracts and now need to find the Journal of Consulting Psychology. Where can you find the call number? (36)

C. You know the name of an author who has done educational research that interests you. How would you proceed in the library in looking for work that this author has done? (37)

D. Discuss the value of direct contact with researchers during a literature review (42).

E. The preschool where you are doing an internship is having difficulties with racial prejudice being expressed among the children. You want to see if there is information available about children and the development of prejudice. Besides going to the reference librarian, describe two other information sources or places in the library where you might reasonably begin your search (be specific).

F. You need to do library research on the Wicky Wacky Test of Motor Ability (WWT). How will you go about finding the information? Be thorough and specific (provide step-by-step description).

G. Briefly discuss the major tools/supports available at the university library for doing research on a behavioral issue.

H. You are assigned to do a research paper on the effects of alcohol on reaction time. Describe the steps that you would follow in your visit to the library. Be specific about the information sources that you would use.

Multiple Choice

1.   In scientific research, reviewing the literature means:
    a. distinguishing between good and poor studies
    b. seeing if earlier studies are repeatable
    c. reviewing textbooks in an area of study
    d. reading general books on a topic
    e. finding out what research has been done previously on a topic (30)

2.   An original research study is most likely to be published in its entirety (the whole study) in:
    a. a book of technical readings
    b. a review article
    c. a technical journal (31)
    d. Social Science Index
    e. the Phychological or Sociological Abstracts

3. A scientific journal that sends all submitted articles to reviewers for their opinions is called a(n) _____ journal.
    a. refereed (31)
    b. specialized
    c. edited
    d. opinionated
    e. basic

4. A book of readings in a specialized area of education is probably a _____ publication.
    a. refereed
    b. non-refereed (31)
    c. non-technical
    d. non-specialized
    e. primary

5. If you wanted to obtain an overview of what was known about aging, you might look first in the:
    a. card catalog
    b. encyclopedia (33)
    c. Psychological Abstracts
    d. Sociological Abstracts
    e. Index Medicus

6. You are seeking a book published by a sociologist in 1957. Probably your first source in a university library should be the:
    a. reference librarian
    b. card catalog (34)
    c. key word directory
    d. inter-library loan desk
    e. Sociological Abstracts

7. If you want to conduct a computer search of the technical literature, you will probably use:
    a. networking
    b. converging operations
    c. key terms (35)
    d. card catalog
    e. megabyte

_____

8. You are looking for recent research on the effects of caffeine on
    problem solving. Probably your first source in the university library
    should be:
    a. technical journal file
    b. periodical room
    c. card catalog
    d. Social Science Citation Index
    e. Psychological Abstracts (36)

9. If you wanted to find all the work done by a psychologist during the last
    few years, you would probably want to go first to:
    a. Psychological Asbtracts (36)
    b. the card catalog
    c. the library stacks where the technical journals   were stored
    d. current periodical room
    e. Encyclopedia of Psychology

10. If you wanted to find other articles that had referred to a psychological
    study that interested you, you would probably look in:
    a. Psychological Abstracts
    b. Social Science Citation Index (37)
    c. Index Medicus
    d. card catalog
    e. Psychological Review

11. A journal you seek is not available in your university library. You
    probably should go next to the:
    a. reference librarian
    b. card catalog
    c. Key Word Directory
    d. inter-library loan desk (40)
    e. Psychological Abstracts

Chapter 4

Essay and Short Answers

A. Compare the use of casual versus systematic observation in behavioral
    research. When would a researcher be likely to use one procedure over
    the other? (48)

B. Discuss the advantages and limitations of systematic observation in
    behavioral research. (50)

C. What is the difference between systematic and participant observation? (48-52)

D. What distinguishes systematic observation from casual observation? (50)

E. Why is systematic observation more desirable than casual observation for the gathering of research data? (50)

F. Discuss methods for measuring and/or improving reliability in systematic observational studies. (53)

G. Discuss the pitfalls (mistakes) to be avoided in observational research. (54)

H. Discuss the value and limitations of participant observation. (55)

I. What is meant by reliability, and how is it taken care of in qualitative observational research? (57)

J. Discuss the stresses upon the observer in field research. (58)

K. When would systematic observation be preferable to participant observation?

L. When would participant observation be preferable to systematic observation?

M. Briefly describe a major strength and a major weakness of observational research.

N. List two (2) advantages and two (2) disadvantages of observation as a research technique.

O. Your seminar in urban sociology has been assigned to do an observational study of garage sales in your community. Describe the steps you would take in carrying out such a study, from the very beginnings to the end. The main issues here are the necessary procedures. You will not know all that you would observe, but how would categories be developed and data obtained? Give all the necessary steps that such a study would require.

Multiple Choice

1. When observation is done <u>without</u> using prearranged categories or a scoring system it is called _____ observation.
   a. unobtrusive
   b. nonreactive
   c. anonymous
   d. casual (48)
   e. participant

2. Which of the following is <u>not</u> a reactive effect from being observed?
   a. people becoming self-conscious
   b. bias on the part of the observer (54)
   c. people attempting to accommodate the observer
   d. influence of the observer's appearance on people's actions
   e. influence of the observer's actions on how people behave

3. Which of the following is <u>not</u> a reactive effect from being observed:
   a. changes in accommodation to the observer during the course of the study
   b. influence of the observer's clothing on the participants
   c. unclear and unreliable scoring categories (54)
   d. people becoming self-conscious and changing their activities
   e. people trying to please the observer

4. In general, observation is a good method for studying:
   a. public behavior (54)
   b. private behavior
   c. opinions
   d. beliefs
   e. all of the above

5. When the observer becomes part of the events being studied, this is called _____ observation.
   a. casual
   b. reflective
   c. systematic
   d. participant (55)
   e. networking

6. The description and study of specific peoples and places is called:
    a. casual observation
    b. photographic memory
    c. ethnography (56)
    d. participant observation
    e. behavioral mapping

7. Ethnography is the study of:
    a. hidden behaviors
    b. public behaviors
    c. individuals over the life span
    d. specific peoples and place (56)
    e. children as they develop

8. Of the various research techniques, one that is most stressful on the investigator and raises the most serious ethical problems is:
    a. participant observation (58)
    b. casual observation
    c. systematic observation
    d. laboratory experimentation
    e. interview

9. _____ is usually a problem in observation.
    a. internal validity
    b. eternal validity
    c. generalizability
    d. reliability (59)
    e. money (research funding)

10. Observation is economical in terms of _____ but expensive in terms of _____.
    a. money . . . equipment
    b. equipment . . . money
    c. time . . . money
    d. money . . . time (59)
    e. time . . . equipment

11. Casual observation is most useful at _____ stages of research:
    a. the beginning (59)
    b. the middle
    c. the end
    d. all
    e. no

12. _____ observation typically creates serious ethical problems:
   a. casual
   b. unsystematic
   c. systematic
   d. ethnographic
   e. participant (59)

Chapter 5
Essay and Short Answers

A. What is behavioral mapping and when would a researcher be likely to use this technique? (62-72)

B. Compare the use and value of place-centered and person-centered behavioral maps. (64-72)

C. Discuss the advantages and limitations of behavioral mapping. (64-72)

D. What are the various types of trace measures and how can they be used in behavioral research? (72-77)

E. Discuss the potential value of systematically studying graffiti in the analysis of street life in a large city such as New York or Stockholm. (72-75)

F. Discuss the advantages and limitations of analyzing trace measures in behavioral research. (72-7)

G. Give an example of a measure of erosion and one of accretion which might be useful in social research. (75-6)

H. The term "nonreactive measures" has been used for research methodologies which sharply reduce or eliminate the likelihood of a participant's being influenced or affected by data collection. Name and briefly describe two (2) research methods which would qualify as "nonreactive."

Multiple Choice

1. Behavioral mapping is a special application of _____ techniques.
   a. interview
   b. experimental
   c. observational (62)
   d. interdisciplinary
   e. qualitative

2. Behavioral mapping is concerned with:
   a. trace measures
   b. private behaviors of individuals
   c. manipulation of variables in the laboratory
   d. observation with prearranged categories
   e. people's behaviors in their environments (62)

3. A study of the places where people spend their time would probably use:
   a. behavioral mapping (62)
   b. casual observation
   c. case study
   d. trace measures
   e. field experimentation

4. A behavioral research technique with considerable relevance for urban design, transportation planning and geography is:
   a. field experimentation
   b. laboratory experimentation
   c. systematic observation
   d. behavioral mapping (62)
   e. trace measures

5. A geographical location linked to customary patterns of behavior occurring over regular time periods is called a(n):
   a. behavioral map
   b. person-centered map
   c. place-centered map
   d. trace measure
   e. behavior setting (62)

6. The laundry room of a housing project and a school auditorium are examples of:
   a. behavioral maps
   b. behavioral networks
   c. behavior settings (62)
   d. mental maps
   e. archival records

7. A chart showing people's locations in space is called a(n):
   a. trace measure
   b. behavior setting
   c. geographic map
   d. behavioral map (63)
   e. trace map

8. In constructing a behavioral map, the researcher can record only those items that:
    a. are observable (63)
    b. are under the researcher's control
    c. remain in the setting after the people have departed
    d. are psychologically important
    e. possess external validity

9. The two major categories of behavioral maps are:
    a. individual and group
    b. casual and systematic
    c. person-centered and place-centered (63)
    d. psychological and geographic
    e. reliability and validity

10. A behavioral map that shows how people arrange themselves within a specific location is called a _____ map.
    a. casual
    b. place-centered (63)
    c. group
    d. locational
    e. person-centered

11. A behavioral map that shows people's movements and activities over a specific period of time is a _____ map.
    a. place-centered
    b. geographic
    c. setting
    d. person-centered (63)
    e. developmental

12. To construct a place-centered behavioral map, researchers:
    a. would employ casual observation
    b. would station themselves in a specific location and observe the action (63)
    c. would chart the behavior of specific individuals over time
    d. would combine observation with interviews
    e. all of the above

13. A detailed analysis of bird droppings would probably be most accurately described as a(n):
    a. experiment
    b. quasi-experiment
    c. trace measures study (69)
    d. case study
    e. experiment-in-nature

14. When a number of place-centered behavioral maps for a specific location have been made, they can be combined into a single _____ map.
    a. people-centered
    b. society
    c. composite (69)
    d. geographic
    e. trace

15. In constructing a person-centered map the researcher's first task is to:
    a. identify the sample and obtain their cooperation (69)
    b. obtain the architect's plans for the setting observed
    c. construct your own diagram of the setting showing all the environmental factors that affect people's behavior
    d. list the behaviors to be recorded
    e. check the reliability of the scoring system

16. Place-centered behavioral maps can be made most easily in:
    a. public locations (72)
    b. hostile environments
    c. private locations
    d. outdoor areas and wilderness
    e. all of the above

17. Lacking legitimate ownership of property, street gangs assert their claim to turf (territory) through graffiti. For researchers, this provides a useful:
    a. person-centered map
    b. place-centered map
    c. erosion measure
    d. trace measure (72-5)
    e. behavior setting

18. The physical remains of interaction after the people have departed are called:
    a. erosion measures
    b. trace measures (75)
    c. composite maps
    d. empty maps
    e. personal space

19. Which of the following is probably not an accretion trace measure?
    a. litter
    b. graffiti
    c. carpet wear (75)
    d. all of the above
    e. none of the above

20. Which of the following is probably an accretion trace measure?
    a. cigarette butts on the ground
    b. graffiti
    c. discarded beer cans
    d. all of the above (75)
    e. none of the above

21. Which of the following is probably an erosion trace measure?
    a. footprints in the snow (75)
    b. graffiti
    c. litter
    d. discarded beer cans
    e. all of the above

Chapter 6
Essay and Short Answers

A. Distinguish between a categorical (discrete) variable and a continuous variable. (83)

B. Define and distinguish between independent, dependent, and extraneous variables. (84)

C. What is meant by the confounding of variables? (First, give the general principle, then give an example.) (84)

D. What are the two common means used to control subject variables when using two or more groups in an experiment? Briefly describe each. (84-5)

E. What distinguishes a <u>control</u> group from an <u>experimental</u> group? (You will need to define each.) (86)

F   Discuss the characteristics of a true (i.e., genuine) experiment. (86)

G. What distinguishes a true (genuine) experiment from a quasi-experiment? Give one or two examples of a quasi-experiment. (88)

H. What is the difference between a laboratory experiment and a natural experiment (quasi-experiment)? (88)

I. Define each of the following terms: continuous variable (83); dependent variable (84); extraneous variables (84); quasi-experiment (88); operational definition (90).

J. What is an <u>operational definition</u>, and why is it important in research? (90)

K. Discuss the benefits and limitations of experimentation as a behavioral research method.

L. What is the difference between <u>casual observation</u> and <u>pilot test</u>? What function does each serve?

M. What does it mean to say that two variables are <u>confounded</u>?

N. Compare and contrast the methods of <u>observation</u> and <u>experimentation</u> with respect to the following: (a) external validity and (b) determination of cause-and-effect relationships.

O. Briefly, describe two different advantages of an observational approach over an experimental approach.

P. The National Board of Health and Safety was concerned about the safety of colored visors in motorcycle helmets. They ran an experiment in which objects (triangles, cubes, squares, spheres) of various colors (red, green, brown, white and gold) were viewed through lenses with the tints used in motorcycle helmet visors. The tints on the lenses were yellow, blue, grey, tan, and clear. The number of errors in color and object identification were scored for each lens tint. 1.) What is the independent variable? 2.) What are the levels (or treatment conditions) of the independent variable? and 3.) What serves as the control condition?

Q. A question of concern to a researcher is whether students in small classes ask more questions than students in large classes. 1.) State this as a hypothesis, and 2.) state the null hypothesis.

R. A philosopher argues that training in logic will improve students' ability to grasp psychological concepts. Others claim that such training, while perhaps of value in other ways, is not particularly relevant to skills in Psychology; and that if there were an improvement it would be attributable to students' paying more attention as a result of the training in logic and believing that it is helpful. In other words, the improvement would be the result of suggestion rather than the training in logic.

Design an experiment (in detail) to shed light (and hopefully resolve) the issue. You do not need to make up the entire instrument, but give an idea of what you would use. Be sure to specify all the necessary components of the study such as selection of subjects, independent and dependent variables, extraneous variables needing control and other important considerations through the selection of a statistical test. (Take time to do a thorough job on this question.)

S. An experiment was designed to investigate the effects of caffeine on problem solving. Students were recruited and randomly assigned to two groups. One group was given regular coffee. The other group drank de-caffeinated coffee. Both groups were told that it was a study of arithmetic ability and that the coffee was provided as a refreshment. About fifteen minutes later, the students were given a test comprised of simple arithmetic problems. Both groups were given the coffee and tested at the same time in the same setting.

Following debriefing of the participants, the tests were scored based on the number of problems solved correctly. The possible scores were 0 to 100. Then the performance of the two groups were compared.

In this study what constitutes the following (be very specific): 1.) subjects 2.) independent variable 3.) dependent variable 4.) treatment group 5.) control group 6.) Is the dependent variable categorical or continuous? and 7.) Do you see any ethical problems with this study? Why or why not?

T. EXPERIMENT: A psychology student wondered if paper color might influence problem solving. So she selected a set of simple arithmetic problems and printed them on blue, pink, and white paper, respectively. Her plan is to present more problems than can be solved by limiting the time to 6 minutes. Then she will compare the number of problems correctly solved on the three colors of paper. Answer the following questions with respect to this study:
1.) What is the independent variable in this study?
2.) What are the levels or values of the independent variable?
3.) What is the dependent variable? 4.) Will the measures of dependent variable be categorical or continuous?

U. State a research hypothesis for the preceding study.

V. What would you expect the results to be if the null hypothesis is correct?

W. The student has access for the first part of the class hour to a group of 300 Psychology 1 students to use as subjects. 1.) How would you recommend that she run the study with respect to assignment of subjects to conditions, i.e., present the basic design with respect to who gets what, when, and how. (For this question, ignore extraneous environmental variables.), and 2.) give your rationale, the reasoning behind your recommendation.

Multiple Choice

1. The research method that is most suited for tracing cause-and-effect relationships is:
    a. experimentation (83)
    b. casual observation
    c. systematic observation
    d. interview
    e. behavioral mapping

2. According to Robert Pirsig in his book, Zen and the Art of Motorcycle Maintenance, an experiment fails when:
    a. the results are ambiguous
    b. the results do not support the hypothesis
    c. the results are not statistically significant
    d. it does not adequately test the hypothesis (83)
    e. all of the above

3. A characteristic or quality that differs in degree or kind and can be measured is called a(n):
    a. subject
    b. variable (83)
    c. value
    d. level
    e. category

4. Age is a _____ variable.
    a. categorical
    b. dependent
    c. subject
    d. object
    e. continuous (83)

5. Gender is a _____ variable.
    a. categorical (83)
    b. dependent
    c. subject
    d. object
    e. continuous

6. For a variable of hair color, blonde, brunette, and red hair would be considered:
    a. subjects
    b. dependent
    c. independent
    d. values or levels (83)
    e. objects

7. The variable that is systematically altered by the experimenter is called the _____ variable.
    a. categorical
    b. continuous
    c. dependent
    d. independent (84)
    e. value or level

8   In an experiment, the treatment condition is the _____ variable.
    a. categorical
    b. continuous
    c. dependent
    d. independent (84)
    e. value or level

9.   In an experiment, the variable influenced by the treatment condition is
     called the _____ variable.
     a. categorical
     b. independent
     c. dependent (84)
     d. continuous
     e. value or level

10. The purpose of an experiment is to:
     a. compare two or more variables as to value or quality
     b. compare the relationship among two or more variables
     c. record behavior using prearranged categories
     d. determine the effects of the independent variable on the
            dependent variable (84)
     e. study behavior in the natural habitat

11. In an experiment, confounding means:
     a. unreliable measurements
     b. apparatus that does not function properly
     c. combining continuous and categorical variables in a single
            experiment
     d. testing the effects of several variables at one time
     e. confusing the effect of the independent variable with the effect of
            other variables (84)

12. In an experiment, variables that are neither the independent nor
     dependent variables are called _____ variables.
     a. invalid
     b. extraneous (84)
     c. unreliable
     d. non-independent
     e. qualitative

13. You conduct an experiment on the effects of alcohol on reaction time.
     You give your subjects 1 or 2 ounces of alcohol. This study uses
     _____ levels of the _____.
     a. one; independent variable
     b. one; dependent variable
     c. two; independent variable (84)
     d. two; dependent variable
     e. three; independent variable.

14. During an experiment, the subject's behavior that is recorded is the _____ variable.
    a. applied
    b. basic
    c. independent
    d. dependent (84)
    e. treatment

15 In an experiment, the presence of _____ variables is a source of error.
    a. independent
    b. dependent
    c. extraneous (84)
    d. continuous
    e. categorical

16. The participants in a behavioral experiment are called:
    a. values
    b. subjects (84)
    c. levels
    d. categories
    e. variables

17. The group treated with or exposed to the different levels of the independent variable is called the:
    a. dependent group
    b. independent group
    c. experimental group (86)
    d. control group
    e. none of the above

18. In an experiment, the group treated with or exposed to the different levels of the independent variable is called the:
    a. dependent group
    b. independent group
    c. anonymous group
    d. matched group
    e. none of the above (86)

_____

19. In an experiment, the group that is deliberately established to be influenced by all of the variables affecting the experimental group except for the independent variable, is the:
a. dependent group
b. control group (86)
c. extraneous group
d. random group
e. none of the above

20. All but one of the following is required for a true experiment?
a. at least two groups or conditions are compared
b. the researcher has control of or can predict and evaluate the experimental treatment
c. the research is conducted in a laboratory (86)
d. subjects are randomly assigned to treatment groups
e. all of the above are required

21. In a field experiment, the researcher:
a. manipulates the dependent variable
b. does not manipulate (change) either the dependent or independent variable
c. does not perform a true experiment
d. manipulates the independent variable outside a laboratory setting (87)
e. does not employ a control group

22. Field experiments often possess more _____ than do laboratory experiments.
a. reliability
b. external validity (87)
c. internal validity
d. controls
e. all of the above

23. In psychology, more experiments are carried out in the _____ than in the _____.
a. laboratory . . . field (87)
b. outdoors . . . indoors
c. natural habitat . . . artificial environments
d. field . . . laboratory
e. natural habitat . . . field

24. As compared with a true experiment, in a quasi-experiment the researcher is unable:
    a. to compare at least two conditions or groups
    b. to use random assignment to treatment groups (88)
    c. to control or predict and evaluate the experimental treatment
    d. all of the above
    e. none of the above

25. Another name for a quasi-experiment is:
    a. natural experiment (88)
    b. true experiment
    c. field experiment
    d. laboratory experiment
    e. qualitative experiment

26. A researcher compares school achievement in two communities having different student-teacher ratios. This is a(n):
    a. true experiment
    b. qualitative experiment
    c. laboratory experiment
    d. reactive experiment
    e. none of the above (88)

27. Because they take place in the real world rather than in the laboratory, quasi-experiments tend to be high in:
    a. internal validity
    b. external validity (88)
    c. internal reliability
    d. external reliability
    e. experimental control

28. A hypothesis is:
    a. an operational definition
    b. a dependent variable
    c. an independent variable
    d. a testable proposition (90)
    e. none of the above

29. When researchers predict that there will be no change in the dependent variable, they have stated a(n):
    a. operational definition
    b. extraneous variable
    c. null hypothesis (90)
    d. pilot test
    e. invalid procedure

30. When a process is defined in terms of the way it is measured, this is called a(n) _____ definition.
    a. dependent
    b. independent
    c. applied
    d. basic
    e. operational (90)

31. Defining something by the means used to measure it is known as a(n) _____ definition.
    a. reliable
    b. valid
    c. convergent
    d. empirical
    e. operational (90)

32. Defining something according to the way it is measured is a(n):
    a. null hypothesis
    b. hypothesis
    c. problem statement
    d. quasi-experiment
    e. operational definition (90)

33. To define intelligence as one's score on an IQ test is an example of:
    a. a null hypothesis
    b. a problem statement
    c. an operational definition (90)
    d. a quasi-experiment
    e. a pilot test

34. Reversing the order of presentation of elements to be judged is called:
    a. the method of converging operations
    b. test-retest reliability
    c. minimal reactivity
    d. reversing
    e. counterbalancing (92)

35. In a study of learning long and short words, both groups receive the same lists of words but in different order. This illustrates the use of:
     a. a null hypothesis
     b. a field experiment
     c. a quasi-experiment
     d. counterbalancing (92)
     e. an operational definition

Chapter 7

Essay and Short Answers

A. What is a behavioral simulation? (96-103)

B. What are the advantages of creating a behavioral simulation of a prison? (96-103)

C. If you were designing a simulation procedure for a physical disability, how would you determine if it were realistic? (98)

D. What are the limitations of using a behavioral simulation of blindness using blindfolded sighted subjects? (103)

E. When would a simulation be preferable to observation or experimentation?

F. What are the major limitations of simulation? (103)

Multiple Choice

1. Behavioral simulations are:
   a. observations of actual situations
   b. case studies of problem situations
   c. imitations of actual situations (97)
   d. a characteristic in quality that differs in degree or kind
   e. used to determine the effects of the independent variable upon the dependent variable

---

2. The chief difference between a simulation and an experiment is that:
   a. an experiment always takes place inside a laboratory
   b. an experiment cannot deal with serious psychological problems
   c. the researcher in a simulation attempts to separate variables that naturally occur together
   d. the simulation is an artificial situation while the experiment is not
   e. experiments separate variables that are connected, while simulation leaves them together (97)

3. In a behavioral simulation:
   a. there is only one variable
   b. there can be more than one variable, so long as each is introduced one-at-a-time
   c. variables are introduced systematically so that their effects can be measured
   d. all of the above
   e. none of the above (97-8)

4. When a behavioral simulation has started:
   a. the researcher controls the flow and pace of events
   b. independent variables are introduced one at a time
   c. it develops its own dynamics and proceeds at its own pace (98)
   d. observation is used in real-world settings
   e. there is no fixed ending time

5. An advantage of using simulation is that:
   a. it is less expensive than constructing an actual object (98)
   b. it is more real than reality
   c. variables are introduced one at a time so that their specific effects can be measured
   d. the effects of air pollution cannot be studied in the laboratory
   e. the researcher becomes part of the situation

6. Simulations are most useful in situations:
   a. where only a single variable is operating
   b. where the researcher is part of the action
   c. when variables cannot be measured
   d. where observation and experimentation are not feasible or ethical (99)
   e. all of the above

7. Simulation should be used as a research method primarily:
   a. when the researcher is part of the action
   b. when only a single variable is operating
   c. because it is more realistic than reality
   d. because people enjoy playing games
   e. when other methods such as experimentation or observation are unavailable or inappropriate (99)

8. The use of slides by landscape researchers to obtain peoples' ratings of landscape quality is an application of:
   a. trace measures
   b. simulation (101)
   c. human factors research
   d. case study
   e. qualitative research

Chapter 8

Essay and Short Answers

A. Define each of the following terms: 1.) manifest content (108); 2.) latent content (109); 3.) probe (120); 4.) unstructured interview (109); 5.) depth interview (111)

B. Compare the advantages and disadvantages of structured and unstructured interviews. When would a researcher be more likely to use one type than the other? (109)

C. Under what circumstances is an <u>unstructured</u> interview more desirable than a structured one (make your answer as complete as possible). (109)

D. Discuss the advantages and limitations of depth interviewing. When is this approach most useful? (111)

E. Briefly describe three (3) different and major considerations to be kept in mind regarding the proper way to conduct an interview. (111)

F. Discuss some of the possible nonverbal cues given by an interviewer that might influence a respondent's answers. (118)

G. Discuss ways in which interviewer bias can be minimized.

H. Discuss the advantages and disadvantages of interviewing as a behavioral research method.

I. How are open-ended responses in an interview dealt with in data analysis? Explain the steps in enough detail so that a new researcher would be able to understand what needs to be done.

J. Briefly describe two (2) different processes or aspects one must pay attention to while conducting an interview (while the interview is in progress).

K. You are sending an assistant out to do some interviews. List five (5) different and important points of advice that you would give that person about the actual conduct of the interview.

L. What is an in-depth interview, and why is it used in research?

M. Describe two (2) research uses for the in-depth interview.

N. Describe two (2) advantages and two (2) disadvantages of interviewing as a method of data collection.

Multiple Choice

1. Probably the best method for exploring complex feelings and attitudes is:
   a. systematic observation
   b. casual observation
   c. face-to-face interview (108)
   d. behavioral mapping
   e. questionnaire

2. Researchers found that laboratory tests were _____ interviews in detecting alcoholism.
   a. less accurate than (108)
   b. more accurate than
   c. as accurate as (same detection rate)

3. During an interview, material which is obvious and conveyed in the spoken information is called:
   a. behavioral information
   b. behavioral content
   c. manifest content (108)
   d. latent content
   e. psychiatric content

4. In an interview, the content that is obvious and conveyed in the spoken information is termed:
   a. structures
   b. unstructured
   c. contextual
   d. latent
   e. manifest (108)

5. In an interview, content which is not directly expressed in words, but is communicated in indirect and nonverbal ways, is called the _____ content.
   a. manifest
   b. Freudian
   c. latent (109)
   d. null
   e. valid

6. During an interview, material which is less obvious and often nonverbal, is called:
   a. case study
   b. behavioral input
   c. nonbehavioral input
   d. latent content (109)
   e. manifest content

7. When the questions are formulated beforehand and asked in a specific order, there is a(n) _____ interview.
   a. structured (109)
   b. unstructured
   c. latent
   d. manifest
   e. depth

8. When the main goals are to explore all the alternatives and define areas of importance to the respondent, the interviewer is likely to use a(n) _____ interview:
   a. standardized
   b. structural
   c. unstructured (109)
   d. psychiatric
   e. behavioral

9. An interview in which the questions are formulated ahead of time and asked in a set order and manner is termed a(n) _____ interview.
   a. latent
   b. open-ended
   c. closed
   d. unstructured
   e. structured (109)

10. In an interview study, the further one moves from a(n) _____ procedure, the greater the likelihood of interviewer bias.
   a. unstructured
   b. in-depth
   c. semistructured
   d. intensive
   e. structured (109)

11. When an interviewer wants to combine information from a large number of respondents, it is probably best to use a(n) _____ interview.
   a. manifest
   b. latent
   c. structured (110)
   d. unstructured
   e. depth

12. An unstructured interview is desirable:
   a. as a preliminary step in developing a structured form for an interview
   b. when the goal is to define issues of importance to the respondent
   c. as part of a qualitative study
   d. all of the above (110)
   e. none of the above

13. If all of the respondents in an interview study are asked the same questions but the order in which the questions are asked is varied, the researcher has used a(n) _____ interview.
   a. structured
   b. unstructured
   c. semistructured (110)
   d. standardized
   e. unstandardized

14. The depth or intensive interview is a special form of the _____
    interview.
    a. structured
    b. standardized
    c. semistructured
    d. field
    e. unstructured (111)

15. When designing an interview, it is generally more effective to have the
    specific questions at the beginning, followed by more general ones.
    a. true
    b. false (112)

16. When an interviewer uses a question or comment to obtain clarification of
    a respondent's answer, this question or comment is called a:
    a. depth charge
    b. depth gauge
    c. nonverbal communication
    d. psychiatric question
    e. none of the above (120)

17. When a respondent during an interview gives an incomplete or unclear
    answer, the interviewer may want to use a(n):
    a. nonverbal cue
    b. probe (120)
    c. judgment
    d. critical response
    e. creative reply

18. The task of classifying interview answers into fixed categories is called:
    a. coding (120)
    b. probing
    c. depth analysis
    d. pacing
    e. creative analysis

19. Interview responses that are written down exactly as they were said are
    called _____ response.
    a. coded
    b. precoded
    c. verbatim (120)
    d. structured
    e. semistructured

20. The interviewer's written descriptions of what the respondent meant are called _____ responses.
    a. unstructured
    b. creative
    c. coded
    d. paraphrased (120)
    e. verbatim

21. Establishing categories of interview responses is called:
    a. coding (120)
    b. probing
    c. verbatim response
    d. depth interviewing
    e. nonverbal communication

22. For their interviews on sexual behavior, Alfred Kinsey and his interviewers recorded people' responses:
    a. verbatim
    b. as paraphrased by the interviewer
    c. subjectively
    d. using mathematical signs and numbers (121)
    e. with creative additions

23. When describing interview results in a report, Sommer and Sommer recommend:
    a. following the sequence of the questions asked during the interview
    b. beginning with the most clear and important results (124)
    c. starting with the most controversial findings
    d. starting with the least controversial findings
    e. none of the above

Chapter 9
Essay and Short Answers

A. When is it desirable to use an open-ended format for a questionnaire? (131)

B. When is it desirable to use a closed (multiple choice) format for a questionnaire? (131)

C. Briefly define each of the following terms: 1.) questionnaire (129); 2.) survey research (129); 3.) open-ended questions (130); 4.) salience (131); 5.) balance (on a questionnaire) (135-6)

D. Distinguish between the <u>format</u> and <u>content</u> of a questionnaire (you will have to define each). (129-131)

E. List three (3) reasons why close-ended questions are desirable in a questionnaire. (131)

F. List three (3) conditions where open-ended questions are preferable to closed questions. (131)

G. Describe the advantages and limitations of mail surveys. (141-2)

H. What are some methods used to increase the return rate in a mail survey? (143-4)

I. Compare the advantages and disadvantages of interviews and self-administered questionnaires. (150)

J. A radio station is interested in students' opinions about its music programming. They come to you for assistance and provide you with three people who will assist you in your research. You decide to develop a questionnaire. <u>What</u> is the first major step you would take in this process of developing the questionnaire, and <u>why</u> is this step important?

K. List the preliminary considerations and steps taken <u>before</u> the actual construction of a questionnaire is made.

L. Evaluate the following for use on an attitude questionnaire: "The United States should abandon its space program and spend the money on domestic programs." Is this an adequate item? Why or why not?

M. List all the things wrong with the following item on a questionnaire for college students: "Do you feel that DSI staff are ignorant and elitist?"

N. List one major advantage of an open-ended question and a major advantage of a closed question.

O. Most people think of questionnaires as being used to gather information about some topic. Describe one other use to which questionnaires are sometimes put. (Scratch paper or something on which to wipe your feet will not count!)

P. Make up one questionnaire item that has at least two (2) flaws. Describe the flaws.

Q. Describe three (3) different circumstances or reasons when a paper-and-pencil questionnaire would be preferable to an in-person interview.

Multiple Choice

1. The systematic gathering of information about peoples' beliefs, attitudes, values, and behavior is called:
   a. a questionnaire
   b. an attitude scale
   c. interview form
   d. a behavioral map
   e. survey research (129)

2. A series of written questions on a topic about which the respondent's opinions are sought is:
   a. a questionnaire (129)
   b. a content analysis
   c. a structured interview
   d. a semistructured interview
   e. a verbatim account

3. In a self-administered questionnaire:
   a. the interviewer asks questions and the respondent fills in the answers
   b. the interviewer asks questions and records the respondent's answers
   c. the interviewer allows the respondent to formulate questions
   d. the respondents fill out questionnaires provided by the researcher (129)
   e. there are no structured questions

4. Which of the following procedures is most efficient in time and effort?
   a. self-administered questionnaire (129)
   b. interviewer-administered questionnaire
   c. structured interview
   d. unstructured interview
   e. semistructured interview

5. In behavioral research, it is difficult to find a more economical method than _____.
   a. the structured interview
   b. the unstructured interview
   c. the questionnaire (129)
   d. systematic observation
   e. participant observation

6. The subject matter of a questionnaire is its:
   a. timing
   b. pacing
   c. content (129)
   d. format
   e. balance

7. The structure and appearance of a questionnaire, including question wording and layout on the page is called:
   a. balance
   b. format (130)
   c. order
   d. face validity
   e. content

8. _____ refers to the importance of an issue in people's minds.
   a. Value
   b. Reliability
   c. Validity
   d. Connotation
   e. Salience (131)

9. An open-ended format on a question is desirable when:
   a. the researcher does not know all the possible answers to a question
   b. the range of possible answers is very large
   c. the researcher wants to avoid suggesting answers to the respondents
   d. the researcher wants answers in the respondent's own words
   e. all of the above (131)

10. On a questionnaire, an open-ended format is desirable when:
    a. there is a large number of respondents
    b. there is a large number of questions
    c. the researcher wants to avoid suggesting answers to the respondent (131)
    d. the answers are to be machine-scored
    e. the responses from several groups are to be compared

11. On a questionnaire, a multiple-choice format is desirable when:
    a. the researcher does not know all the possible answers to a question
    b. there is a large number of respondents and questions (131)
    c. the range of answers to a question is very large
    d. the researcher wants to avoid suggesting answers to the respondents
    e. the researcher wants answers in the respondent's own words

12. _____ refers to the importance of an issue in people's minds.
    a. Balance
    b. Salience (131)
    c. Format
    d. Content
    e. Open-mindedness

13. Asking people to rank order items in terms of importance is a good way to determine the _____ of opinions.
    a. balance
    b. structure
    c. depth
    d. salience (131)
    e. format

14. A questionnaire format in which answer headings are presented at the top and listing the items at the side is called a:
    a. depth question
    b. salient question
    c. open-ended question
    d. balanced distribution
    e. matrix (132)

15. The neutrality of a questionnaire can be improved through proper
    _____ of items.
    a. depth
    b. balance (135)
    c. salience
    d. coding
    e. structure

16. The first draft of a questionnaire will need:
    a. reliability
    b. validity
    c. coding
    d. revision (136)
    e. pacing

17. Sommer and Sommer recommend that a questionnaire should begin
    with:
    a. factual, noncontroversial questions (137)
    b. the most important questions
    c. the most controversial questions
    d. the most specific questions
    e. none of the above

18. In constructing a questionnaire, general questions on a topic should
    _____ specific questions.
    a. precede (137)
    b. follow
    c. be perfectly balanced with
    d. be mixed together with
    e. cancel out

19. The best way to reduce ambiguity in wording items on a questionnaire
    is through:
    a. balance
    b. coding
    c. pretesting (138)
    d. content analysis
    e. all of the above

20. A disadvantage of a mail survey is:
    a. impersonality
    b. low return rate
    c. slowness
    d. financial cost
    e. all of the above (142)

21. In comparison with a personal interview, a questionnaire is less satisfactory for respondents who are:
    a. very young children
    b. very old
    c. on the move
    d. infirm
    e. all of the above (150)

Chapter 10
Essay and Short Answers

A. Compare the Thurstone and Likert-type attitude scales in terms of format, methods of construction, and utility. (131-6)

B. Compare the advantages and disadvantages of the Thurstone and Likert-type attitude scales. Why is the Likert-type much more frequently used today? (156-8)

C. Describe the steps necessary to construct a Thurstone-type attitude scale. (156)

D. Describe the steps necessary to construct a Likert-type attitude scale. (157)

E. Describe three (3) methods for testing the reliability of an attitude scale. (159-60)

F. An educational researcher has constructed a scale to measure student attitudes toward a proposed compulsory driver education course. How could the validity of the scale be tested? (159)

G. Describe some of the problems and limitations in the use of attitude scales. (160)

H. Describe the semantic differential and how it can be used in a study of student attitudes toward residence hall environment. (160-3)

I. Describe the advantages and limitations of the semantic difference. When is its use <u>not</u> recommended? (163)

J. Describe the problems and limitations of performance rating scales in research studies. (165)

K. What is sensory evaluation and how is it used in industry to develop new food products? (167-9)

L. Describe the value and the limitations of sensory evaluation procedures. (167-9)

M. Briefly define each of the following: 1.) graphic rating scale (153); 2.) comparative rating scale (154); 3.) Thurstone-type attitude scale (156-8); 4.) Likert-type attitude scale (157-9); 5.) split-half method (159); 6.) semantic differential (160f); 7.) sensory evaluation (167f); 8.) double-blind procedure in research (169)

Multiple Choice

1. A _____ represents a series of ordered steps at fixed intervals used as a standard of measurement.
    a. survey
    b. balance
    c. questionnaire
    d. scale (153)
    e. coding sheet

2. When a respondent to a questionnaire is asked to place marks along a continuous line, this is a(n) _____ scale format.
    a. attitude
    b. Thurstone-type
    c. graphic rating (153)
    d. Likert-type
    e. survey

3. A(n) _____ scale requires the rater to select one of a graded series of intervals.
    a. attitude
    b. step (154)
    c. graphic rating
    d. employee rating
    e. product rating

4. On a _____ scale, the respondent is asked to compare the applicant with others in the same category.
   a. comparative rating (154)
   b. graphic rating
   c. step
   d. Thurstone-type
   e. Likert-type

5. An attitude scale is constructed so that all of its questions:
   a. concern several controversial issues
   b. cover both controversial and noncontroversial issues
   c. concern a single issue (154)
   d. allow people to make their answers at any point along the line
   e. are of equal emotional impact

6. The psychologist who wrote the article, "Attitudes can be Measured," which was considered very radical when it was published in 1928, was:
   a. Charles Osgood
   b. L. L. Thurstone (156)
   c. R. Likert
   d. U. Bronfenbrenner
   e. F. D. Becker

7. The first step in constructing a Thurstone-type attitude scale is to:
   a. collect statements on a topic from people who hold clearly positive or negative opinions
   b. ask judges to rate statements on a topic as to favorability or unfavorability
   c. ask people to check only those statements with which they agree
   d. collect statements on a topic from people holding a wide range of attitudes (156)
   e. identify groups or organizations known to have strong opinions on the topic

8. On a Thurstone-type attitude scale given to respondents, the statements should be placed:
   a. in random order (156)
   b. beginning with the most favorable
   c. beginning with the least favorable
   d. beginning with the most controversial
   e. beginning with the least controversial

9. In a _____ scale each item has a weight based upon judges' evaluation of favorability or unfavorability. The respondent (person doing the rating) simply checks the statements with which he or she agrees. The weights of the agreed-with terms are added up to give an overall score.
   a. Thurstone-type (156-7)
   b. performance
   c. Likert-type
   d. semantic differential
   e. performance rating scale

10. During the construction of a Thurstone-type attitude scale:
   a. the judges indicate their personal agreement with statements on an 11-point scale ·
   b. the judges indicate their personal agreement with statements on a 6-point scale
   c. the judges rate each statement as to potential ambiguity
   d. the judges rate each statement as to clarity
   e. the judges do not indicate their personal opinions on the issue (156-7)

11. In filling out a Thurstone-type scale:
   a. a respondent indicates degrees of agreement with items
   b. respondents do not rate neutral items
   c. place a check mark next to all items
   d. respondents do not indicate strength of agreement or disagreement with each item (156-7)
   e. none of the above

12. A statement receives a score of 3.2 on a 20-item attitude scale. This is probably a _____ scale.
   a. Likert-type
   b. Thurstone-type (156-7)
   c. semantic differential
   d. mixed-type
   e. performance rating

13. A Likert-type scale does not include items which are:
   a. positive
   b. negative
   c. neutral (157)
   d. too controversial
   e. none of the above

14. The respondent's score on a Thurstone-type scale is:
    a. the average rating from all the items on the scale
    b. the sum of all the items checked
    c. the sum of all items with which the person agrees minus the sum of items which the person disagrees
    d. the sum of the weights of all statements checked divided by the number of statements checked (157)
    e. none of the above

15. A Likert-type attitude scale includes:
    a. only statements that are clearly favorable or clearly unfavorable (157-8)
    b. only statements that can be scored as five or zero
    c. statements covering all degrees of opinion on an issue
    d. both ambiguous and nonambiguous statements
    e. all of the above

16. A respondent receives a score of 46 on a 20-item attitude scale. This is probably a _____ scale.
    a. Likert (158)
    b. Thurstone
    c. mixed
    d. balanced
    e. Osgood

17. On a _____ scale, respondents are asked to check their degree of agreement or disagreement with all statements on the list.
    a. semantic differential
    b. performance rating
    c. sensory evaluation
    d. Thurstone-type
    e. Likert-type (158)

18. Compared with the Thurstone-type attitude scale, the greater _____ of the Likert-type makes it more attractive to researchers.
    a. reliability
    b. validity
    c. simplicity (158)
    d. attractiveness
    e. none of the above

19. A common method for testing the <u>validity</u> of an attitude scale is to:
   a. administer it to the same group on two occasions
   b. divide the items into halves and correlate them
   c. administer it to a random sample of the population
   d. administer it to people known to hold strong opinions on both sides of an issue (159)
   e. eliminate all the items on which there is a wide range of opinion

20. The _____ of an attitude scale is the degree to which it measures what it is supposed to measure.
   a. validity (159)
   b. reliability
   c. salience
   d. consistency
   e. average scale value

21. A measure of reliability in which the same test is given to the same person on two occasions is the _____ method.
   a. test-retest (159)
   b. internal reliability
   c. equivalent forms
   d. content analytic
   e. split-half

22. Consistency in measurement is called:
   a. validity
   b. reliability (159)
   c. balance
   d. scale
   e. performance

23. What are the common methods for testing the reliability of an attitude scale?
   a. test-retest
   b. split-half
   c. equivalent forms
   d. all of the above (159)
   e. none of the above

24. When an attitude scale is given to the same person twice and the results are compared, this is the _____ method for determining reliability.
    a. scale comparison
    b. split-half
    c. test-retest (159)
    d. equivalent forms
    e. multimethod

25. When an attitude scale is divided into two parts which are then compared, this is the _____ method for determining reliability.
    a. scale comparison
    b. interval
    c. split-half (159)
    d. test-retest
    e. equivalent forms

26. When two different scales on a topic (Forms A and B) are constructed, and peoples' scores on the two forms are compared, this is the _____ method for determining reliability.
    a. split-half
    b. test-retest
    c. equivalent forms (159)
    d. scale comparison
    e. fixed interval

27. If you wish to test the reliability of the observations made by two observers or of two forms of a test, the statistic you will need to calculate is probably a:
    a. Chi Square
    b. Analysis of Variance
    c. Correlation Coefficient (160)
    d. t-test
    e. percentile

28. The semantic differential procedure was developed by:
    a. Laud Humphries
    b. Charles Osgood (160)
    c. Rensis Likert
    d. L. L. Thurstone
    e. R. Gifford

29. What type of scale is illustrated below:
    good ___:___:___:___:___ bad
    strong ___:___:___:___:___ weak
    a. Likert-type
    b. matrix type
    c. Thurstone-type
    d. semantic differential (160)
    e. performance rating

30. The connotations of things or the meanings of concepts are measured by:
    a. a Likert-type scale
    b. sensory evaluation
    c. a Thurstone-type scale
    d. a performance rating scale
    e. the semantic differential (161)

31. The semantic differential is a good instrument for exploring:
    a. complex attitudes
    b. simple attitudes
    c. the physical characteristics of things
    d. the connotative meaning of things (161)
    e. the reliability of measurement

32. In the research that developed the semantic differential, three major categories of meaning were identified. These were:
    a. test-retest, equivalent forms, and split-half
    b. favorable, unfavorable, and undecided
    c. images, maps, and percepts
    d. value, activity, and strength (161)
    e. height, volume, and length

33. In evaluation research, the _____ dimension of the semantic differential is of most importance.
    a. value (161)
    b. activity
    c. strength
    d. desire
    e. reliability

34. The tendency to make ratings of specific abilities on the basis of an overall impression is called:
    a. dissimilation
    b. pygmalion effect
    c. halo effect (164)
    d. stimulus generalization
    e. Hawthorne effect

35. The tendency to make ratings of specific abilities on the basis of an overall impression is called a(n):
    a. stimulus error
    b. observer error
    c. halo effect (164)
    d. experimenter bias
    e. covert paradox

36. The reluctance of raters to say unkind things about people limits the usefulness of _____ in research.
    a. the semantic differential
    b. performance rating scales (164)
    c. attitude scales
    d. sensory evaluation
    e. halo effects

37. _____ is the relationship between the physical qualities of objects and their sensory attributes.
    a. Semantic meaning
    b. Performance rating
    c. Consumer research
    d. Attitude research
    e. Psychophysics (167)

38. During sensory evaluation, when people are presented items two at a time and asked to compare them, this is the method of:
    a. test-retest
    b. alternative forms
    c. parallel forms
    d. paired comparison (168)
    e. standards

39. During sensory evaluation, when the respondent is not aware of the origin or identity of the item rated, this is called a(n):
   a. halo effect
   b. experimental error
   c. experimenter bias
   d. blind trial (169)
   e. unpaired comparison

40. During sensory evaluation, when neither the respondent nor the experimenter is aware of what is being tasted, this is a(n):
   a. experimenter error
   b. blind taste trial
   c. double blind taste trial (169)
   d. biased experiment
   e. unplanned comparison

Chapter 11
Essay and Short Answers

A. Discuss the utility (value) of content analysis in social science research. (176-7)

B. What are the advantages of content analysis when compared with other approaches to printed material? (176-7)

C. Discuss the advantages and didsadvantages of content analysis as a research tool. (176-182)

D. Describe the sequence of steps to be undertaken in a content analysis of magazine advertisements. (176-182)

E. Discuss the importance of reliability in content analysis. How can reliability be measured or improved? (181)

F. List and describe two (2) different advantages and two (2) different disadvantages of content analysis as a research technique. (176-182)

Multiple Choice

1. A content analysis is:
   a. a technique for mapping or charting behavior
   b. a technique for determining what people want or need
   c. a technique for determining people's likes and dislikes
   d. a series of steps used to develop a standard of measurement
   e. a technique for systematically describing the form and content of written or spoken material (176)

2. The format (illustrations, location, number of pages, etc.) constitutes the _____ of material used in content analysis.
   a. manifest meaning
   b. structure (176)
   c. content
   d. latent meaning
   e. specific topics or themes

3. Content analysis has been used most often in studies of:
   a. attitudes
   b. performance
   c. the mass media (176)
   d. behavior over time
   e. connotative meaning

4. The basis of a content analysis is:
   a. a behavioral map
   b. intergroup ratings
   c. quantification (176)
   d. intergroup comparisons
   e. multimethod approach

5. Expressing something in numbers is termed:
   a. interpretation
   b. explanation
   c. qualification
   d. description
   e. quantification (176)

6. In a content analysis of printed materials, <u>structure</u> refers to:
   a. specific topics
   b. general themes
   c. gender of the figures shown
   d. location on the page, format, etc. (176)
   e. cost of the research

7. Content analysis allows a person to do social research without:
   a. coming into contact with people
   b. laboratory equipment
   c. checking with a human subjects committee
   d. expensive facilities
   e. all of the above (176)

8. In using _____, the researcher has no effect on the material analyzed.
   a. content analysis (176)
   b. systematic observation
   c. experimentation
   d. behavioral mapping
   e. survey research

9. The materials for a content analysis will probably be found in:
   a. a laboratory
   b. an outside area for real-world observation
   c. a library or newspaper file (176-7)
   d. people's private spaces
   e. a collection of behavioral maps

10. Of all the methods discussed in <u>A Practical Guide to Behavioral Research</u>, content analysis scores the highest marks in _____.
    a. validity
    b. possibilities for replication (177)
    c. practical utility
    d. cost
    e. all of the above

11. The results of a content analysis are:
    a. purely descriptive (181)
    b. valid
    c. highly reliable
    d. cost-effective
    e. explanatory

Chapter 12
Essay and Short Answers

A. Discuss the value or utility of diaries in behavioral research. What are their drawbacks or limitations? (160-4)

B. Discuss the value of life histories in behavioral research. What are their disadvantages or limitations? (160-4)

C. What are the problems in making a systematic content analysis of personal documents? (164-5)

D. How can archival measures be used in social science research? What are their advantages and disadvantages? (165-8)

E. Describe the problems in using available public records and statistics in social science research. (165-8)

F. What is a victim survey? Include in your answer, its purpose and how it is done. (166)

Multiple Choice

1. Behavior that is private and takes place inside the home can often be studied best through:
   a. systematic observation
   b. casual observation
   c. questionnaires
   d. behavioral mapping
   e. diaries (184)

2. When one writes an account of one's own life, it is termed a(n):
   a. autobiography (186)
   b. case study
   c. content analysis
   d. biography
   e. self analysis

3. An account of one person's life as seen by another person is called a(n):
   a. fictionalized account
   b. autobiography
   c. case study
   d. biography (187)
   e. novel

4. The most common use of autobiographies in behavioral research is to:
   a. illustrate findings that have been established through other methods (187)
   b. test hypotheses from the laboratory
   c. validate the results of observational studies
   d. produce quantitative information suitable for content analysis
   e. validate behavioral maps of individuals

5. The use of private documents in social research was pioneered by:
   a. L. L. Thurstone
   b. W. I. Thomas (188)
   c. R. Likert
   d. Charles Osgood
   e. N. F. R. Russo

6. _____ are public records and documents.
   a. Diaries
   b. Biographies
   c. Case studies
   d. Archives (189)
   e. Content analyses

7. Information overload is most likely for the researcher using:
   a. autobiographies
   b. systematic observation
   c. experimentation
   d. content analysis
   e. archival records (189)

8. A method used to correct for the under-reporting of crime is:
   a. content analysis
   b. victim survey (190-1)
   c. interviews with criminals
   d. analysis of census records
   e. archival research

9. The use of census data or other social statistics to study characteristics of groups is called:
   a. social survey research
   b. aggregate data analysis (191)
   c. life history approach
   d. group biographical research
   e. group content analysis

Chapter 13

Essay and Short Answers

A. Unusual events call for unusual research techniques. Discuss the relevance of this statement in regard to research on natural disasters. (195)

B. What are the benefits and limitations of the case study? (195, 200)

C. What distinguishes a case study from other research methods; that is, what is a case study? (195)

D. Discuss the methods that can be used in gaining cooperation of local residents for a case study of a rural community. (197-8)

E. How can reliability be checked in a case study? (198-9)

F. What are the strengths and weaknesses of a case study?

G. What factors distinguish a case study from a journalistic account of an event in a newspaper? (Be sure to include a definition of a case study in your answer.)

Multiple Choice

1. A researcher studies the effects of an earthquake that devastated a Japanese city. He collects questionnaires from a thousand people and personally interviews 200 residents about their actions. The study is best described as a(n):
   a. experiment
   b. experiment in nature
   c. case study (195)
   d. attitude investigation
   e. mail survey

2. A case study:
   a. provides an opportunity for a controlled experiment
   b. offers the chance to conduct before-and-after observations
   c. is a technique for systematically describing the form or content of written material
   d. keeps the researcher from interfering with the subject matter
   e. none of the above (195)

75

3. Making an in-depth study of a person is to the Gallup poll as a(n):
   a. interview is to an observation
   b. questionnaire is to an interview
   c. case study is to a survey (195)
   d. archival study is to an experiment
   e. experiment is to a case study

4. In selecting an event or subject for case study, most researchers have selected:
   a. commonplace things that can be generalized across settings
   b. commonplace things that cannot be generalized across settings
   c. unusual and newsworthy things (195)
   d. the lives of ordinary working people
   e. private events

5. In a case study, _____ is one means of assessing reliability.
   a. balanced items
   b. human subjects committee approval
   c. cross-checking accounts from different observers (198)
   d. all of the above
   e. none of the above

6. The case study emphasizes:
   a. generalization across settings and participants
   b. the systematic analysis of multiple occurrences
   c. questionnaires in group sessions
   d. the uniqueness of the participants and the setting (200)
   e. none of the above

Chapter 14
Essay and Short Answers

A. Discuss the major uses of cameras and recorders in behavioral research. (205-8)

B. Describe some of the problems in using cameras and recorders in behavioral research. (205-8)

C. What are the <u>disadvantages</u> of using a tape recorder for an interview? (121)

Multiple Choice

1. An apparatus for presenting visual material in timed exposure is called a
   a. reaction time tester
   b. neon daylight tube
   c. time lapse camera
   d. tachistoscope (202)
   e. videotape cassette recorder

2. Laboratory research almost always requires:
   a. a videotape camera
   b. a tachistoscope
   c. a reaction time tester
   d. special equipment or apparatus (204)
   e. psychological tests

3. The most common use of a camera in behavioral research is to:
   a. present materials to subjects
   b. obtain original data
   c. make illustrations for talks and presentations
      (211-2)
   d. gain the goodwill of respondents
   e. provide a check on human observers

4. The main problem in using a video camera to obtain original data is that:
   a. the machine is likely to break down
   b. transcribing the data is tedious and cumbersome (210)
   c. it is difficult to learn to operate the controls
   d. the machine is heavy and cumbersome
   e. it is difficult to estimate light values in the field

Chapter 15

Essay and Short Answers

A. Describe the sequence of steps used in constructing a standardized test. (219)

B. Briefly define each of the following terms: 1.) projective test (220-1); 2.) test validity (214-5); 3.) item analysis of a test (219); 4.) individually administered IQ test (215-6); 5.) test norms (214)

Multiple Choice

1. The most useful tests in psychological research are:
   a. valid
   b. reliable
   c. standardized
   d. all of the above (214)
   e. none of the above

2. A psychological test is _____ to the extent that we know what it measures or predicts.
   a. valid (214)
   b. reliable
   c. standardized
   d. all of the above
   e. none of the above

3. _____ refers to the stability of test measurement over time.
   a. Validity
   b. Reliability (214)
   c. Standardization
   d. Split-half
   e. Projectivity

4. A _____ test has norms which can be used in interpreting results.
   a. valid
   b. reliable
   c. standardized (214)
   d. projective
   e. all of the above

5. A standardized test is likely to have:
   a. a test manual
   b. normative data (test norms)
   c. reliability information
   d. validity information
   e. all of the above (214)

_____

6. _____ will disclose how a person's test score compares with others having taken the same test.
   a. Reliability information
   b. Norms (214)
   c. Validity information
   d. Split-half comparisons
   e. Test-retest comparisons

7. To determine a person's academic level, you would probably use a(n) _____ test.
   a. school achievement (215)
   b. group IQ test
   c. individual IQ test
   d. occupational interest test
   e. specialized ability test

8. To obtain a detailed picture of a person's intellectual abilities, primarily for clinical use, you would probably use a(n) _____ test.
   a. school achievement
   b. group IQ
   c. individual IQ (215)
   d. clinical
   e. personality

9. To measure how a person's intelligence compares with others of the same age group, you would probably use a(n) _____ test.
   a. school achievement
   b. group IQ (215)
   c. individual achievement
   d. clinical
   e. specialized ability

10. Which of the following tests could be administered by a relatively untrained person:
   a. individual IQ test
   b. group-administration IQ test (216)
   c. clinical test
   d. projective test
   e. individual personality test

11. The Modern Language Aptitude Test measures:
    a. school achievement
    b. intelligence
    c. personality
    d. occupational interests
    e. specialized abilities (216)

12. Standardized tests developed to identify patterns of behavioral dysfunction are of the _____ test type.
    a. achievement
    b. intelligence
    c. personality
    d. clinical (216)
    e. occupational interest

13. To measure interest in vocation (job types) you would probably use a(n) _____ test.
    a. school achievement
    b. group IQ
    c. occupational interest (216)
    d. specialized ability
    e. individual IQ

14. To identify patterns of behavioral dysfunction (behavioral problems), you would probably use a(n) _____ test.
    a. mood
    b. individual intelligence
    c. specialized ability
    d. clinical (216)
    e. interest

15. The first step in constructing a standardized test is to:
    a. define the performance to be measured (218)
    b. collect potentially useful test items
    c. check previous research
    d. conduct a pilot study
    e. check reliability

16. A(n) _____ shows the degree to which the various test items "hang together" or cluster.
    a. validity check
    b. pilot test
    c. item analysis (219)
    d. test norm
    e. performance analysis

17. The Rorschach inkblot test is a(n):
    a. mood test
    b. projective test (220)
    c. general interest test
    d. individual interest test
    e. vocational guidance

18. A test in which the respondent gives a subjective description about a vague stimulus such as a drawing or photograph is called a(n) _____ test.
    a. personality
    b. aptitude
    c. projective (220-1)
    d. standardized
    e. achievement

19. The TAT and the Rorschach are examples of _____ tests.
    a. aptitude
    b. projective (220-1)
    c. intelligence
    d. achievement
    e. occupational interests

20. _____ tests use questions or items that are deliberately vague or incomplete.
    a. Mood
    b. Personality
    c. Specialized ability
    d. Individual IQ
    e. Projective (220-1)

21. A major shortcoming of standardized tests is that:
    a. they are difficult to obtain
    b. they lack reliability
    c. they seldom fit specific research needs (221)
    d. they lack validity
    e. the answers are obvious to the respondent

22. The research value of projective techniques is limited by:
    a. their high cost
    b. the long time spent in administering these tests
    c. their low reliability (221)
    d. communication problems in administration
    e. use of group administration

Chapter 16

Essay and Short Answers

A. Briefly define each of the following terms:
   1) sampling error (225)
   2) sampling bias (225-6)
   3) stratified sample (227-8)
   4) purposive sample (228-9)

B. Define sampling error and sampling bias? How can they be estimated or reduced in survey research? (225)

C. Define and distinguish between sampling error and sample bias. (225)

D. Describe three (3) types of nonprobability samples. How can their validity be increased? (228)

E. Define each and indicate when a quota sample is preferable to a random sample. (228)

F. Discuss those factors entering into the decision as to how large a sample is needed. (229-31)

G. Describe three (3) different factors for a researcher to consider when deciding on sample size. (229-31)

_____

H. (Read the entire question before writing your answer): a) Define and distinguish between a stratified sample and a quota sample; b) when would the latter (quota sample) be preferable?; and c) what are its (quota sample) limitations?

Multiple Choice

1. In survey research, the entire group of people in a category is called a:
   a. stratified sample
   b. random sample
   c. quota sample
   d. purposive sample
   e. population (225)

2. A sample is used to make generalizations about the _____ from which it was drawn.
   a. quota
   b. methodology
   c. population (225)
   d. sampling error
   e. random variation

3. In survey research, the smaller group that is selected to receive questionnaires in the mail is called a(n):
   a. population
   b. sample (225)
   c. quota
   d. random error
   e. systematic error

4. The degree to which a survey sample differs from the population is termed:
   a. error (225)
   b. quota
   c. random variation
   d. bias
   e. systematic variation

5. Even when a research study is properly executed, you do not expect the sample to be exactly like the population from which it is drawn. This is because of:
   a. systematic sample drift
   b. sampling error (225)
   c. sample bias
   d. entropy
   e. population inconstancy

6. The two general sources of error in survey research are:
   a. random and systematic variation
   b. random and quota bias
   c. probability and randomness
   d. sample and population
   e. sampling error and sampling bias (225)

7. In survey research, sampling error can never be _____ but it can be _____.
   a. average . . . estimated
   b. estimated . . . averaged
   c. eliminated . . . estimated (225)
   d. estimated . . . eliminated
   e. known . . . eliminated

8. A common method for reducing sampling error is to:
   a. tighten up the procedure
   b. eliminate bias
   c. increase sample size (225)
   d. increase randomness
   e. increase population size

9. _____ samples are those in which we know the probability for the inclusion of any given individual.
   a. Probability (226)
   b. Nonprobability
   c. Population
   d. Nonpopulation
   e. Unbiased

10. In _____ sampling, every person in the entire population has an equal likelihood of being selected.
    a. biased
    b. stratified
    c. random (226)
    d. quota
    e. probability

11. Visiting a high school and interviewing every third person in the courtyard is not likely to yield a _____ sample of the student body.
    a. random
    b. stratified
    c. probability
    d. all of the above (226)
    e. none of the above

12. Which of the following is considered as a type of probability sample?
    a. quota sample
    b. stratified sample (227)
    c. purposive sample
    d. accidental sample
    e. all of the above

13. A(n) _____ sample is selected so that its characteristics are proportionate to those present in the total population.
    a. random
    b. stratified (227)
    c. quota
    d. accidental
    e. purposive

14. Which of the following would not be considered a type of nonprobability sample?
    a. quota
    b. stratified (227)
    c. purposive
    d. accidental
    e. snowball

15. A researcher wishes to assess opinions about feminism in a psychology class of 100 people—60 women and 40 men. He puts the names of all the women in one hat and does the same for the men with another hat. He selects the names of six women and four men to be interviewed. This is a _____ sample.
    a. random
    b. stratified (227-8)
    c. quota
    d. convenience
    e. purposive

16. In a _____ sample, the likelihood of selection is not actually known.
    a. random
    b. stratified
    c. probability
    d. nonprobability (228)
    e. all of the above

17. In a(n) _____ sample, the selection categories are specified according to the needs of the investigator rather than the numbers in the population.
    a. random
    b. accidental
    c. probability
    d. quota (228)
    e. all of the above

18. A(n) _____ sample is one in which key individuals are specifically targeted for the research.
    a. probability
    b. representative
    c. quota
    d. accidental
    e. purposive (228)

19. In a(n) _____ sample, the researcher asks respondents for the names of other people to contact.
    a. quota
    b. stratified
    c. accidental
    d. random
    e. snowball (228)

_____

20. When the independent variable has a strong and clear effect on the dependent variable, a(n) _____ sample can be used.
   a. accidental
   b. volunteer
   c. smaller (228)
   d. larger
   e. qualitative

Chapter 17
Essay and Short Answers

A. Mr. Smith gave his 4th grade class a spelling test. The mean for the group was 41 and the standard deviation was 3. On the next test, the mean was the same, but the standard deviation was 6. What does that tell us in general about the distribution of scores on the second exam relative to the first one? (242-3)

B. Two different distributions of scores have the same means (Mean = 4) but different standard deviations. S.D. = 2 for Distribution A, and S.D. = 5 for Distribution B. In one sentence what is the difference between these two distributions? (And it does not count to simply say that the standard deviations are different.) (242-3)

C. The following is a frequency distribution of scores on a spelling test. Calculate the mean and the median. (Ans: Mean = 5.54, Median = 5)

f	X
0	10
0	9
1	8
2	7
3	6
5	5
1	4
1	3
0	2

D. A class received the following scores on a research methods exam: 50, 50, 40, 60, 30, 55, 35, 30, 50, 55.
   1) Summarize these data in a frequency distribution: be sure to label X and f.
   2) Why would anyone care about a standard deviation?
   3) Under what circumstances will the mean, median, and mode of a frequency distribution be identical? (250)

E. In describing a set of scores or measures, such as exam scores or income figures, what statistic or statistics would you use to describe the group as a whole—to describe its central characteristics?
1) State your choice(s).
2) Give the reasons for your selection.

F. Calculate the requested statistics for the frequency distribution below.

X	f
8	1
7	0
6	2
5	5
4	2
3	1

N   = _____ (Ans: 11)
ΣX = _____ (Ans: 56
Mean   = _____ (Ans: 5.09)
Median = _____ (Ans: 5)
Mode   = _____ (Ans: 5)

1) Present the data from the frequency distribution above in cumulative frequencies (a table, not a graph).
2) Draw a bar graph for the distribution above. Be sure to label the axes.

G. In the preceding situation, what would you use to convey information about the spread or disperson of scores within the group?
1) State your choice(s).
2) Give the reasons for your choice(s).

H. These are scores on a color blindness test given to a group of employees.

Number of errors	Frequency
0	15
1	2
2	2
3	0
4	1
5	0
6	0
7	0

1) What is the median?   (Ans: 0)
2) What is the mode?   (Ans: 0)
3) What is the range?   (Ans: 4)
4) What is the mean?   (Ans: .5)

I. Here are scores from a class given a test of hearing performance.

Number of errors	Frequency
0	0
1	1
2	0
3	2
4	9
5	10
6	6
7	1
8	0
9	1
10	0

1) What is the median score?   (**Ans:** 5)
2) What is the mode?   (**Ans:** 5)
3) What is the range?   (**Ans:** 8)
4) What is the mean?   (**Ans:** 4.83)
e. What is the N?   (**Ans:** 30)

Multiple Choice

1. The firsthand or initial scores on a psychological test are considered:
   a. test scores
   b. inferential statistics
   c. measures of variability
   d. central tendencies
   e. raw data (233)

2. You are interested in seeing if political parties vary with respect to numbers of male and female members. Using political party (Republican or Democratic) as your independent (predictor) variable, you find out the figures for the number of men and women. In this circumstance the <u>dependent variable</u> is:
   a. categorical (234)
   b. continuous
   c. nonexistent
   d. Republican
   e. Democratic

3. In analyzing data from a class given an IQ test, the number of times each score occurs constitute the:
   a. raw bits
   b. data bits
   c. frequencies (234)
   d. cumulative percentage
   e. central tendency

4. In a frequency distribution, X stands for:
   a. unknown quantity
   b. raw data
   c. frequency
   d. number of cases
   e. raw score (234)

5. In a frequency distribution, f stands for:
   a. categorical measures
   b. frequencies (234)
   c. means
   d. interval grouping
   e. number of cases

6. In a frequency distribution, N stands for:
   a. number of cases (234)
   b. number of categories
   c. central tendencies
   d. continuous measures
   e. categorical measures

7. When the cumulative frequency is divided by the total number of cases and multiplied by 100, it becomes the cumulative:
   a. distribution
   b. score
   c. percentage (236)
   d. bar graph
   e. polygon

8. Which of the following would most likely not be considered a categorical measure?
   a. gender
   b. county of residence
   c. political party affiliation
   d. age (236)
   e. nation of birth

---

9. Which of the following is <u>not</u> a type of average:
   a. mean
   b. median
   c. mode
   d. cumulative percentage (236)
   e. all of the above

10. The _____ is the arithmetic average.
    a. standard deviation
    b. mode
    c. frequency distribution
    d. mean (239)
    e. median

10. The midpoint of a distribution when all the test scores are arranged from highest to lowest is called the:
    a. median (212)
    b. central axis
    c. standard axis
    d. numerical equator
    e. mean

11. Which is the correct formula for the mean?
    a. ΣX

    b. $\dfrac{\Sigma X}{N}$ (239)

    c. $\dfrac{\Sigma X (100)}{N}$

    d. $\dfrac{\Sigma X}{100}$

    e. $\dfrac{f}{X}$

---

12. Which is the correct formula for the mean computed from a frequency distribution of scores?

   a. $\dfrac{\Sigma X^2 - \dfrac{(\Sigma X)^2}{N}}{N}$

   b. $\dfrac{\Sigma X}{N}$

   c. $\dfrac{\Sigma (Xf)}{N}$ (240)

   d. $f(X)$

13. Which is the correct formula for the median?
    a. highest minus lowest score

   b. ΣX

   c. $\dfrac{\Sigma X}{N}$

   d. $\dfrac{\Sigma X}{2}$

   e. none of the above (240-1)

14. The midpoint of a distribution when all the test scores are arranged from highest to lowest is called the:
    a. median (240-1)
    b. central axis
    c. standard axis
    d. numerical equator
    e. mean

15. In a set of scores, the most frequently-occurring score is referred to as the:
    a. standard deviation
    b. median
    c. mean
    d. mode (242)
    e. range

16. The single score that occurs most frequently in a distribution is called the:
    a. standard deviation
    b. interval
    c. median
    d. mode (242)
    e. mean

17. In a frequency distribution, the measure of central tendency that is easiest to compute is the:
    a. interval
    b. standard deviation
    c. mean
    d. mode (242)
    e. median

18. The most commonly used measures of variability are the:
    a. median and mode
    b. range and interval
    c. frequency and interval
    d. range and standard deviation (242)
    e. mean and median

19. Of the three major measures of central tendency, the one that is least informative is the:
    a. mean
    b. median
    c. mode (242)
    d. frequency
    e. range

20. The _____ is an indicator of variability, of how spread out the scores in a distribution are.
    a. Chi square
    b. standard deviation (242)
    c. median
    d. mean
    e. percentile

21. The _____ provides a quick and easy assessment of variability.
    a. range (242)
    b. mean
    c. median
    d. mode
    e. standard deviation

22. A small standard deviation indicates that most scores are grouped around the:
    a. range
    b. mean (242)
    c. frequency
    d. mode
    e. interval

23. $\sqrt{\dfrac{\Sigma X^2 - \dfrac{(\Sigma X)^2}{N}}{N}}$ is the formula used to compute the:

    a. median
    b. range
    c. standard deviation (242)
    d. frequency distribution
    e. cumulative frequencies

Chapter 18

Essay and Short Answers

A. Hermoine Harper administered a preference test of healthfood items to an equal number of boys and girls. Each child received a score reflecting the number of items preferred. For example, Inge had a score of 12 and Heinz had a total of 6.
   1) What statistic should Hermoine calculate in order to determine whether there was a significant difference between genders in health food preference scores? (**Ans:** t-test for independent groups)
   2) State the null hypothesis in Hermoine's study.
   3) If Hermoine's resulting statistic had a probability of less than .01, what would she conclude and why?

B. A bicycle organization advocates the wearing of protective helmets in the belief that this practice reduces the severity of injury or likelihood of death. They develop a 20-point continuous scale for assessing injury (ranging from 1, no injury, to 20, death). Then they compare 50 accident cases where a helmet was worn against 50 in which it was not. Assume that the extraneous vairables are being either controlled or accounted for in some appropriate manner. Now they come to you for advice.
   1) Think through what their data might look like, and then select the statistical test you would advise them to use in testing their hypothesis. (**Ans:** t-test for independent groups)
   2) What is the basis for your choice?

C. Researchers Jones and Li claimed that coordination in boys shows a decline at the time of the pubescent growth spurt (height increase). They selected a sample of 13 year old boys, none of whom had begun the growth spurt. The boys were tested on a series of coordination measures which yielded a single composite score for each individual. The growth patterns of the boys were followed, and when each reached a specified rate of accelerated growth, he was retested on the same coordination tasks. State the null hypothesis for this study

D. After the follow-up, the means for the coordination measure were calculated. The mean for Before Growth was 34.3 (out of a possible 50). The mean During Growth was 31.2. Select the appropriate statistical test of this difference. (**Ans:** t-test for matched scores)

E. Their statistical test yielded the following result: t=3.41, df=40. 1.) Give the probability associated with their result, using the appropriate statistical notation (use the appropriate table in the book appendix). 2.) What should they conclude? State clearly in 1 or 2 sentences.

F. As a research project, a student compared two (2) groups of students: blondes and brunettes. On a scale of conservatism, where the higher the score, the more conservative the attitude, the blondes had a mean score of 47 and the brunettes scored 30.
1.) What statistical test is appropriate here? (**Ans:** t-test for independent groups)
2) Give the reason(s) for your choice.

G. In a comparison of study methods, a class was randomly divided into two groups. One group studied individually, and the other group studied in pairs. On the exam, Group 1 (individuals) had a mean score of 64, while the mean for Group 2 (pairs) was 73. A t-test was done, and the result was t=3.04, p<.01. Setting aside the statistical meaning, what can you conclude (i.e., what would you tell your 16-year-old brother)?

H. Statistical tests are used to test the null hypothesis. Assume you have done an experiment testing a new teaching technique against a traditional one. You apply the appropriate inferential statistics (in this case a t-test between means), and based on the outcome, you reject the null hypothesis. The probability level of your statistic (the t-ratio) was less than .01 (p < .01). In clear English, what does this mean?

I. A Psychology student wondered if paper color might influence problem solving. She selected a set of arithmetic problems and printed them on blue, pink, and white paper. After running the study, she obtained the following results:

Pink paper - mean number of problems solved = 36
Blue paper - mean number of problems solved = 39
White paper - mean number of problems solved = 43

1) What statistical test should she run in order to evaluate the significance of these differences? (**Ans:** ANOVA)
2) Give the reason(s) for your choice.

J. Twenty-one students were selected to take a course designed to improve their study techniques. Before taking the course, they were given material to study, and then examined on it. That was Test A (highest possible score = 100). At the end of the course, a similar exam was given to find out if the course had a beneficial effect. The second exam is Test B (also 100 points possible). The mean for Exam A was 62, and for exam B, the mean was 79. Answer the following questions.
1) What type of statistical test would you use to evaluate the difference? (**Ans:** t-test for matched scores)
2) What table in the appendix would you use to find the probability level of the statistic generated in (a) above? (**Ans:** Critical values for t-test)
3) What is the df? (**Ans:** 20)
4) Assume that the difference is statistically reliable. What conclusion would you draw (in plain English, <u>not</u> statistical jargon).

K. In the preceding study, a Pearson product-moment correlation between Test A and Test B resulted in r = .592.
1) What table in the appendix would you use to find the probability level of this statistic?
2) Using that table, what do you conclude about the statistical significance of the findings? Is it significant or not? If so, what is the probability level?
3) Explain the findings in clear English - what does it mean regarding performance on Test A and Test B?
4) Relate this finding to the conclusion drawn from the mean scores (see preceding question). What does the correlation add? (Point is to get at difference in information provided by means and by correlations.)
5) If the correlation had been .003, what would you conclude about the relationship?

L. A movie critic rated films on a score of 1 (very poor) to 7 (excellent). A correlation of .92 was obtained between his ratings and the cost of the individual movies. In plain English, what does this mean?

M. Draw a scattergram for the following data (be sure to label the axes):

Amount of ice cream sold (thousands of gals)	Number of drownings
10	2
12	5
15	8
14	7
13	6

N. Correlation - read both questions before answering.
   1) Give an example (okay to make it up if it sounds reasonable) of a negative correlation. Be sure to describe why the relationship is that of a negative correlation.
   2) Draw a graph illustrating the preceding. Be sure to properly label the axes.

O. What is the range of possible values that the Pearson Product Moment Correlation Coefficient may take? (Ans: -1.0 to +1.0)

P. In a popular magazine, a researcher claimed that the use of oral contraceptives and IUDs had contributed to the increase in the divorce rate. He based his conclusion on solid evidence of an increase in contraceptive use and in an increase in the incidence of divorce. He went on to suggest that having young children in the home reduced the immediate likelihood of divorce. This is all the information that was presented. As a student of research methodology, what comment would you make about this study and its interpretation?

Q. A count was made of the number of male and female bicycle riders who either stopped, slowed only, or raced through an intersection with a stop sign. The following results were obtained:

Gender	Stopped	Slowed	Raced
Male	20	15	10
Female	6	14	19

You apply the appropriate inferential statistics (in this case Chi square) and come up with df = 2, $\chi^2 = 9.8$. The probability level of that statistic is less than .01 ($p < .01$). Answer the following questions clearly:
   1) What is the null hypothesis in this study?
   2) What is meant by $p < .01$ (remember, explain clearly).
   3) Would you accept or reject the null hypothesis?
   4) What conclusion would you draw from the study (be precise).

R. Testing the hypothesis that Californians are taller than New Yorkers, Kyo was able to gain access to a sample of each and divided them into two categories: above average (using the median height for the U.S. as the cutoff), and equal to or below average. He found 10 Californians equal to or below average and 60 above average. There were 25 New Yorkers below average and 20 above average in height.
1) What statistical test is appropriate here? (**Ans:** Chi-square)
2) Give the reason(s) for your choice.

S. You have made a count of the number of males and females in different age groups who patronize the Dairy Queen. You wonder if there are more people in one group than another, compared with what you would expect by chance. For example, are there more female teenagers or male prepubescents, in contrast with adults of either sex? What statistical tests would you use? (**Ans:** Chi-square)

T. A fellow student asked the question, "What will you be doing in 5 years?" to a sample of seniors majoring in engineering, and to another sample of seniors majoring in philosophy. He coded their answers into three categories: specific job, general occupational area, and don't know. He wants to find out if there was a difference in these between the engineers and philosophers.
1) What statistical test is appropriate here?
2) Give the reason(s) for your choice.

U. A researcher studied the images of minority group members shown on television and obtained the following results in a content analysis.

Occupational status	Ethnic status	
	Minority	Non-minority
Professional (white collar)	14	53
Nonprofessional (blue collar)	49	20

$\chi^2 = 34.192$ (assume this is correct)
Answer the following questions:
1) What is the df?
2) Using the appropriate table in the appendix, what value must the obtained χ^2 exceed in order to be significant at the .01 level?
3) In clear language, what can you conclude about the results (be specific).

Multiple Choice

1. Inferential statistics permit generalizations from:
   a. description to explanations
   b. samples to populations (248)
   c. quantity to quality
   d. quality to quantity
   e. hypothesis to test

2. The prediction that the independent variables will have no effect on the dependent variable is called the:
   a. sampling error
   b. sampling bias
   c. population error
   d. null hypothesis (248)
   e. alternative hypothesis

3. Following a statistical test of the null hypothesis, the rejection of the null hypothesis means:
   a. there is no reliable difference
   b. there is a reliable difference (249)
   c. there is a reliable difference but it is not important
   d. the sample is skewed
   e. the procedure is biased

4. The statement that the independent variable will have a significant effect on the dependent variable is called the:
   a. alternative hypothesis (249)
   b. probability level
   c. significance level
   d. sampling error
   e. reliability effect

5. The notation, $p < .01$, means that the probability of the obtained result:
   a. representing a true difference is less than 1 out of 100
   b. representing a true difference is less than 1 out of 10
   c. representing a true difference is less than 1 out of 5
   d. being due to chance is less than 1 out of 100 (249)
   e. being due to chance is less than 1 out of 5

----

6. p < .05 means that the probability of the null hypothesis:
   a. being true is less than1 out of 20 (249)
   b. being false is less than1 out of 20
   c. being true is less than1 out of 100
   d. being false is less than1 out of 100

7. Another name for probability level is:
   a. alternative hypothesis
   b. null hypothesis
   c. sampling error
   d. inferential statistic
   e. level of significance (249)

8. The notation p < .05 is called the:
   a. .05 alternative hypothesis
   b. .05 null hypothesis
   c. .05 chance difference
   d. .05 level of significance (249)
   e. .05 level of variance

9. The two most common statistical tests for continuous data are:
   a. p < .05 and p < .01
   b. sampling error and sampling bias
   c. t-test and Chi square
   d. Chi square and analysis of variance
   e. t-test and analysis of variance (250)

10. The t-test is used for comparing:
    a. inferential and descriptive statistics
    b. continuous and categorical measures
    c. means and medians
    d. differences between two groups (250)
    e. differences between two or more groups

11. When there are many extreme scores at the upper or lower ends of a distribution of scores, the distribution is described as:
    a. skewed (250)
    b. biased
    c. null
    d. alternative
    e. not working

_____

12. _____ is a statistical test used to assess the reliability of
differences between means.
   a. Pearson product-moment coefficient
   b. t-test (250)
   c. Chi square
   d. percentile rank
   e. Spearman Rank-order Coefficient

13. The scores from people who have been tested before and after an
experimental treatment are called _____ measures:
   a. biased
   b. skewed
   c. correlated (252)
   d. independent
   e. categorical

14. Analysis of variance is used for comparing:
   a. observed and expected differences
   b. differences within categorical data
   c. significance with probability levels
   d. differences among two or more groups (255)
   e. continuous with categorical data

15. _____ can be used to measure the effects of more than one
variable at a time.
   a. ANOVA (255)
   b. t-test for matched groups
   c. t-test for independent groups
   d. all of the above
   e. none of the above

16. When an ANOVA test involves more than one independent variable, it is
called a _____ design.
   a. null
   b. probability
   c. categorical
   d. continuous
   e. factorial (259)

17. _____ is a statistical test for categorical data.
    a. t-test for independent groups
    b. t-test for matched groups
    c. ANOVA
    d. all of the above
    e. none of the above (260)

18. The Chi-square test becomes unreliable when:
    a. some of the observed frequencies are small
    b. some of the expected frequencies are small (263)
    c. the data are skewed
    d. the data are categorical
    e. the data are continuous

19. An association between two sets of scores shows:
    a. causation
    b. correlation (264)
    c. bias
    d. a positive relationship
    e. a negative relationship

20. When an increase in one variable is accompanied by an increase in the other variable, this is:
    a. causation
    b. bias
    c. skew
    d. a positive relationship (264)
    e. a negative relationship

21. A perfect positive correlation between two variables produces a correlation coefficient of:
    a. 0
    b. +1.0 (264)
    c. +10.0
    d. +100.0
    e. -1.0

22. As one variable increases, the other decreases. This is called a:
    a. null finding
    b. null hypothesis
    c. positive relationship
    d. negative relationship (264-5)
    e. causation

23. Correlation does not prove:
    a. causation (265)
    b. association
    c. relationship
    d. all of the above
    e. none of the above

24. When both sets of scores are continuous, probably the best coefficient to use is:
    a. r (265)
    b. rho
    c. χ^2
    d. M
    e. XY

25. Assume that on the STAI (State-Trait Anxiety Inventory) we found a correlation of -.87 (p < .01) between anxiety level and exam score. We would conclude that within the class:
    a. as anxiety increased, exam performance declined (265)
    b. as anxiety increased, exam performance improved
    c. there was no relationship between anxiety and exam performance
    d. anxiety scores ranged from low to high but there were no significant differences within the group on exam scores
    e. exam scores ranged from low to high but there were no significant differences within the group on anxiety

26. The Pearson product-moment coefficient (r) _____ influenced by extreme scores in a distribution.
    a. is strongly (265)
    b. is slightly
    c. is not

27. The Spearman Rank-Order Coefficient is more useful than the Pearson Product-Moment Coefficient:
    a. when one set of scores is continuous
    b. when both sets of scores are continuous
    c. when there is no relationship between two sets of scores
    d. when there is a strong positive association between two sets of scores
    e. the data are not normally distributed (265)

28. Under most circumstances, the most stable and reliable measure of correlation is:
    a. χ^2
    b. ANOVA
    c. r (269)
    d. rho
    e. t

29. Briefly define the meaning of each of the following common statistical notations. (270)
    a. SD
    b. χ^2
    c. p
    d. rho
    e. $(\Sigma X)^2$
    f. ΣX^2
    g. N
    h. X
    i. $\overline{X}$
    j. ANOVA
    k. df
    l. t
    m. $p < .01$

30. In the left column, indicate the correct statistical notation for each of the following terms: (270)
    a. rho   Spearman rank-order coefficient
    b. SD or σ standard deviation
    c. $\overline{X}$ or M   arithmetic average
    d. ΣX sum of all the individual scores
    e. ANOVA or F   analysis of variance
    f. χ^2 Chi square
    g. p   probability
    h. >   greater than
    i. $p < .05$ probability less than .05
    j. r   Pearson product-moment coefficient
    k. ΣX^2 sum of squares
    l. N   number of scores

Chapter 19

Essay and Short Answers

A. Briefly define the meaning of these common notations found on many calculators. Note that in many cases they are also common statistical notations (275)
1) X
2) X^2
3) ΣX^2
4) σ
5) $\sqrt{}$
6) F
7) r or CORR
8) STO
0) RCL

B. Write the common notations for these keys found on statistical calculators.
1) sum of squares (SS or ΣX^2)
2) standard deviation (σ, S, or S.DEV)
3) Pearson product-moment correlation coefficient (r or CORR)
4) Chi square (χ^2)
5) Variance or square of the standard deviation (Var, σ^2, or S^2)
6) square root of a number ($\sqrt{}$ or $\sqrt{X}$)

Multiple Choice

1. On a hand calculator, when a symbol is written above rather than on a key, this usually means, if you want to use the upper symbol:
   a. the key must be pressed twice
   b. the key must be pressed lightly
   c. this is an alternative meaning of the lower symbol
   d. a separate function button must be pressed first
       (274)
   e. the symbol above has been replaced by a newer
       meaning

2. SPSS-X, Minitab, BMDP and SAS are examples of:
   a. main frames
   b. types of computers
   c. types of calculations
   d. statistical programs (277)
   e. common statistical notations

----

3. When coding missing data for computer processing, the best procedure is to first:
   a. eliminate the case from the sample
   b. assign a randomly-selected number
   c. check the program requirement for missing values
      (278-279)
   d. leave the response blank
   e. code the response as zero

4. When using a computer for data analysis, a codebook is necessary for:
   a. repairing computer hardware
   b. statistical analyses
   c. understanding computer software
   d. running a computer program
   e. keeping track of variable names and value levels
      (278-279)

Chapter 20
Essay and Short Answers

A. Describe the information you would find in each of the major sections of an article using APA-style.

B. Imagine that you are going to give a spoken presentation at a scientific meeting. Discuss some of the things you would pay attention to in preparing your talk.

Multiple Choice

1. Most American journals in psychology require authors to use the style manual of the:
   a. American Psychological Association (284)
   b. American Psychiatric Association
   c. American Library Association
   d. International Psychological Society
   e. Social Science Citation Index

2. At the beginning of a technical article is a brief summary. This is called the:
   a. acknowledgment
   b. preface
   c. review
   d. abstract (287)
   e. author's note

3. In a scientific paper, the literature review will most likely be found in the:
   a. acknowledgment
   b. preface
   c. introduction (287)
   d. procedure
   e. discussion

4. In a published journal article using APA style, the first section is the:
   a. appendix
   b. results
   c. abstract (287)
   d. introduction
   e. references

5. The _____ is the section of a journal article in APA style that most people are likely to read.
   a. results
   b. conclusions
   c. introduction
   d. references
   e. abstract (287)

6. In APA style, the _____ contains a statement of the problem, its theoretical and practical significance, and its place in a larger body of knowledge.
   a. conclusions
   b. introduction (287)
   c. results
   d. title
   e. abstract

7. In APA style, the abstract for a journal article:
   a. should not exceed 150 words (287)
   b. should be around a full typed page, double-spaced (320 words)
   c. should be only a single sentence
   d. should be almost two typewritten pages
   e. is placed at the end of the article text, but before the references

8. In actual practice, the abstract of a technical article is written by the author _____ the rest of the article is completed.
   a. before
   b. at the same time
   c. after (287)

9. The _____ section of a journal article describes specifically what was done.
    a. introduction
    b. method (287)
    c. results
    d. conclusions
    e. discussion

10. Tables and charts will most often be found in the _____ section of a journal article.
    a. introduction
    b. method
    c. results (288)
    d. discussion
    e. conclusions

11. In writing a research report, speculation about the meaning of the findings should be:
    a. left out of a scientific report
    b. included in the introduction section
    c. included in the discussion section (289)
    d. included in the results section
    e. included in the methods section

12. If there are opinions stated in a scientific article, they will probably be found in the:
    a. abstract
    b. results
    c. introduction
    d. discussion (289)
    e. method

13. The last section of a technical report is most likely to be the:
    a. results
    b. references
    c. conclusions
    d. appendix (291)
    e. running head

14. In a technical report, the _____ contains material not essential for understanding the report.
   a. results
   b. discussion
   c. introduction
   d. appendix (291)
   e. method

Chapter 21
Essay and Short Answers

A. Discuss the likely timetable after an article is submitted to a technical journal in a field such as social psychology. (298-9)

B. Describe the advantages and drawbacks of the following methods for disseminating (making available) the findings from a research study.
   1) article in scientific journal
   2) news release
   3) talk at a professional meeting

Multiple Choice

1. When a paper has been accepted for publication in a social science journal, you can expect to see it in print within six months.
   a. true
   b. false (198-299)

2. A copy of an accepted journal article that is circulated before publication is called a:
   a. draft
   b. reprint
   c. news release
   d. page proof
   e. preprint (300)

3. The time-consuming process by which scientists critically evaluate each other's work is called a:
   a. literature search
   b. submission fee
   c. peer review (303)
   d. critical analysis
   e. content analysis

_____

4. <u>All but one</u> of the following applies to giving a talk at a meeting. Select the inappropriate answer.
   a. Leave time at the end for questions
   b. Write out your talk word for word (304)
   c. Practice your talk on friends or colleagues
   d. Check out the setting beforehand
   e. Use audiovisual aids

Final Examination Questions

1. The Costingmore Publishing Conglomerate (CPC) hired four professors, three professional writers and two artists, to produce what they consider a knockout introductory Psychology textbook. You are a Dean at a small undergraduate college and have considerable power around the place. You taught Psychology in the past but now another professor teaches the subject. The CPC representative has been pushing the new textbook claiming that it is much better than textbook X which your college now uses in its introductory class of about 120 students, taught in three sections of about 40 students each.
Design a study to evaluate CPC claim including the following.
   a. Name your method and give the reasons for your choice.

   b. Design the study (assume as Dean that you will have access to needed resources) describing the method (subject, instruments, procedures, etc.), and describe how the results would be analyzed.

2. Researcher Schnerd was interested in the effects of birth order (position in family, i.e., first-born, second-born, last-born, etc.) on performance in mathematics (measured by latest course grade). She decided to study high school students and posted a sign-up sheet outside of the library at the local high school. Students who signed up were telephoned and asked about their birth order and their grade in their last math class. She then compared the grades of the first-born, with those of the second-borns and third-borns, with a fourth category including the remaining later-borns. Consider problems of <u>confounding</u> and of sampling and describe what is wrong with this study. Specify each flaw and explain why it is a problem. (<u>Note</u> you lose points if you overlook a serious problem, but you will <u>also</u> lose points if you describe a pseudo-problem, that is, mention something that really isn't a threat to the validity of the study.)

3. Henrik Niit has become very concerned about stories of violence in the household newspaper and is considering a change in subscription, but first wants to determine whether or not the change to the other local paper would reduce the exposure of the kids to bad news. Assuming that subscription rates and service are comparable, what research method would you suggest to him in solving the problem? Briefly explain the method and give the reasons for your choice.

4. A park in your community has been designated for renovation. The City Planner wants it to be changed in ways beneficial to the residents of the area where the park is located. She would like information about people's likes and dislikes, and how they are likely to use the park, for example, for themselves, or for children, or for community-wide events, etc. You offer to do the job for a reasonable fee.
   a. Specify the type of study you would do to answer the questions raised, and give the reasons for your choice.
   b. Describe your mechanism of sample selection, again, stating your reasons.
   c. Outline the general steps that you would take in doing the study, from the beginning to the data gathering point.

5. You are interested in dreams and want to do a study of what people dream about. Design a study which involves at least two research methods covered in this course. It may be one study utilizing two methods, or may be two distinct studies using different research methods but focusing on the same problem.

6. Donna Garcia, a graduate student, is interested in the relationship between personality variables and reactions in emergency situations. For example, do people who have a schizoid temperament respond more quickly and objectively than those who are more neurotic (anxious)? She plans to measure personality variables with the CPI (California Personality Inventory).
   What method would you suggest for getting a reaction to emergency issues?
   a. Name the method and give your rationale (reasons for your choice). (NOTE: You do not need to design the study.)
   b. What are the tradeoffs? That is, the strengths and weaknesses of the suggested method.

7. The Kavitee Kandie Kompany chemistry department has developed a new secret ingredient. Some members of the board of directors think it is wonderful, while others claim that it doesn't make any difference at all in the candy. As a member of the research staff at Kavitee, your job is to design an experiment to answer the concerns of the board of directors. Describe in detail what you would do (design the study, number of subjects, etc.). Also, be sure to specify your hypothesis, the independent and dependent variables, and necessary operational definitions, as well as necessary controls.

8. Many people are interested in the effects of color on people's mood and feelings, for example, is blue more likely to induce feelings of calm than red? What about purple and green? Does one produce more feelings of cheerfulness than the other? You decide to make a comparison of two different, but commonly-used colors used in public buildings, private offices, and homes, to see their effect upon emotion. The colors are Creamy White (CW) and Pastel Green (PG).
Briefly outline two different research techniques you would use to tackle the question of differences produced by these colors on people's emotions. Use the following guidelines for each study.
   a. Name the research technique, and justify your choice.
   b. Describe or outline how you would develop such techniques or instruments, or where you would find them. Do not actually give all the details here—indicate the directions the research would take. In other words, for each method, list the general steps which would be necessary in designing the study.
   c. Who would you sample (from what population), and why?
   NOTE: Be sure to do each of the above for both designs.

9. A student is interested in doing a research project on anorexia nervosa. She heard that you were taking a course on research methodology and comes to you for advice. Because time and resources are limited, she would probably have to limit the study to the local community. She wants to focus more on actual behavior (particularly eating and food-related behaviors.
   a. What research method would you suggest, and why is your method the most preferable?
   b. Describe how you would go about the actual study, i.e., its design. Be clear and specific so that someone else can follow your directions.
   c. Now that you have designed your study, what are its limitations?

---

10. Before Jack Swill, a college sophomore, purchased contact lenses, everyone told him how wonderful they were. Afterwards, people told him all their troubles in wearing them. He guessed it was because he had become a fellow sufferer. He really wondered what peoples' experiences were with respect to contact lenses and what problems they experienced. He would like to do some original (his own) research and has come to you for advice. (He'll even pay you a bit for it, so you want to give him useful and professional advice.)
Read all of the following questions before you begin writing your answer.

    a. What research method would you suggest, and why is your method the most preferable?
    b. What steps would he need to take in setting up the study? Be clear and specific so he will know what to do.
    c. What would you advise him regarding the population to use, and why?
    d. How should he select a sample? What type of sampling would you recommend and why?

11. You are working in a special school for disturbed children and want information from parents about the children's behavior at home, i.e., activity level, cooperation, obedience, problem behavior, etc. You would like this material to be as objective as possible. There are 20 children in the school. You have one month to work on the project, although this is in addition to some ongoing duties at the school

How would you accomplish this assignment? In your answer consider the following:

    a. What method or methods would you select and why?
    b. Give all the necessary steps in doing this study.
    c. Describe the type of data you would obtain, including whether it would be categorical or continuous.
    d. Specify what statistics you would use, indicating the necessary descriptive statistics or comparisons you would want to make.
    e. Discuss the possible use and generalizability of your results.

12. Quan Nguyen has a grant to study problems with hospitals near earthquake faults. He is interested in analyzing the interactions between people and buildings. A major question is, "How is the design of a hospital building likely to affect the reactions and behavior of the staff in the case of an earthquake?" To put it another way, the researcher would want to find out how hospital staff members behave in earthquake conditions, in order to then suggest what design features should be incorporated into hospital buildings. Nguyen has hired you as his research consultant. Answer the following questions (think them through first):
    a. What research method would you suggest, and why is your method the most preferable?
    b. Describe how you would go about the actual study, that is, its design (you needn't discuss issues of obtaining permission and access).
    c. Now that you have designed your study, what are its limitations?

13. You are working in an elementary school and you have come upon an improved procedure for teaching basic arithmetic concepts--that is, you think it is an improvement. The children most likely to benefit are 8 to 10-year olds. You want to see if the procedure works. As a student of Psychology, you also know that many factors affect performance such as attention from adults, motivation, novelty, etc. Design an experiment for testing the teaching procedure. You have about 60 children at each grade level (8 to 10-year olds would most likely be in grades 3 to 5). Use the following as a guide:
    a. Give all the necessary steps you would need to take in order to carry out your study, e.g., state the hypothesis, specify your variable, and proper controls, etc.
    b. Describe the type of data you would get, i.e., continuous or categorical.
    c. Specify the type of statistical analysis you would use on your results, indicating the necessary descriptive statistics and comparisons you would want to make.

14. You are taking a Developmental Psychology course, and for your term project, you decide to study youngsters and video arcades. You are interested in finding out why they go there, how often, how much they spend, etc.
    a. Specify the type of study you would do, e.g., interview, experiment, survey, observation, etc., and give the reasons for your choice, and
    b. Outline the general steps that you would take in doing the study, from the beginning to the data gathering point.